THE POWER OF KNOWING HOW

APPLY THE PRINCIPLE,
GET THE RESULTS!

NIKKA A. WILLIAMS, MSW

THE POWER OF KNOWING HOW
Apply the principle, Get the results!

All scripture quotations are taken from the King James Version of the Bible.

© All rights reserved. In accordance with the U.S. Copyright Act of 1976, scanning, uploading, and electronically sharing any part of this book without permission of the publisher is unlawful piracy and theft of the author's intellectual property. If you would like to use material from the book (other than for review purposes), prior written permission may be obtained by contacting the author. Thank you for supporting the author's rights.

Published by:
www.gogrowandglow.com
nikka@gogrowandglow.com

ISBN 978-1-7339467-0-4

Published in the United States

Special Dedication and Acknowledgements

I truly thank and praise my Lord and Savior, Jesus Christ. For the Lord's love for me and His dedication and faithfulness to me, I am humbled and truly grateful. With Jesus at the helm of my life and sitting on the throne of my heart, I can do all things. My heart's desire and eternal prayer is: Lord, help me to be all You have called me to be. My heart's desire is to live a holy, sanctified life and to please the Lord. Thank you, Lord Jesus, for saving me and giving me a chance at an abundant life and for teaching me how to obtain it.

I am acknowledging all my loved ones in this, my first project, so that when others follow, they will all already know that I love them without mentioning them. So, here we go ...

MY FAMILY ...

*This book is dedicated to my father, **Sanstrick R. Williams**, and my mother **Joyce Ann Williams**. They were my first teachers of the Lord and my first teachers of life's lessons. The time, love, discipline, and sacrifice they invested in me are the foundation on which I stand today. My dad has passed on, and I often wonder whether he would be proud of me if he* were still here. My mom says he most certainly would be. Mom, thank you for loving me enough to introduce me to Jesus. I admire you, and I love you to life. Thank you for believing in me.

My Grandparents ...

In loving memory of my grandparents, **Philip & Elenora Yasper Williams** and **Sarah Louise Bryant**, who have passed on. Thank you for your contributions to my life. May you rest in peace.

My Siblings ...

Magnolia Williams Gittens, I thank you for your love and support of me. Your fierceness and feistiness are true attributes of us Williams girls. 'Til we meet again, ... may you rest in peace.

Koreen Stout, your quiet and meek demeanor, coupled with your sweet spirit, is something I've always wanted to emulate. Your Caribbean flair is so beautiful! I love you.

Sandra Pemberton, I love you so much. You have been such a wonderful support. You are so kind and considerate, and you give of yourself without reservation. Thank you for always being there and listening. You always offer support and kind words that give life. Thank you for keeping us together.

Meedil Williams, my brother, you have been a strong protector and a listening ear. Thank you.

Derrick Bryant, my hero! Derrick, I love you so much. I try to tell you every chance I get, and I feel that I do not tell you enough. You are the best big brother in the world and my real live superhero. You are my Silver Surfer! You have ALWAYS been there for me … from the days of Queens Bridge. I admire you for beating the odds in your life, and I thank you for being one of my biggest supporters. Derrick, YOU ROCK!

Pamela Renee, girl, I love you. You are my she-ro! From the time I came home from the hospital as a baby up until now, you have loved me and protected me. You have always been a strong fighter and an overcomer! I honor you for beating the odds and coming out on top. It is now your time to take care of you and fight for your own life. May the rest of your life be the best of your life!

My Nieces and Nephews …

Antoine, Reggie, Ohenio, Santrice, Jermaine, Tasha, Jeffrey, Santrick, Rosie, Amanda, Chelsea, Nigel, Jehron, Sharae, Nykema, and **Naquay**, I love you all. Thank you for respecting me as your Aunty and believing in the God in me. I further thank you for receiving the advice and counsel I share with you. I love ALL of you, and as I often tell you, Aunty is here for you.

My Uncles and Aunts …

Uncles: **JC, Pattin', Mesha, Glen, Warren,** and **Lloyd** (May All of you rest in peace). Uncles: **James Bryant, Jr. , William Henry, Leamon Earl, Curtis Marcus, Lunsford,** and **Galdo**. Aunt: **Una Horton** (rest in peace). Aunts: **Carolyn Rae, Averricia (Ritza) Mary Ruth,** and **Joyce**. My family is huge, and the blessing for me in this is I had this village to raise me.

My Cousins ...

To all my cousins, thank you for your wisdom, guidance, direction, and examples in life. Your support of my life has been impeccable.

My Church Family...

Pastor Patricia Ann Hayden Newton and **my Agape church family**, *forever my pastor and mentor. Thank you for pushing me to be great! Rest in peace.*

To God be the glory for a church that preaches and teaches the pure, unadulterated word of God and knows how to get a prayer through! My church is a true example of the heart of God and loves to win souls for the kingdom. Thank you,

Bishop Derrick D. Farmer, D.D., and Elect Lady Janice Farmer, *for the patience, time, and effort you have given me. When I wanted to know how much God loved me, you showed up in my life. Thank you for supporting my dreams and goals and always encouraging me to go forward. Thank you for teaching and preaching the Apostolic doctrine and, most importantly, living it and being an example of true holiness.*

Elder Steadley Mothersill and **Evangelist Juanita Mothersill**, *thank you for being examples for me. I love you to life. Elder, you are a living miracle and true man of God. Thank you for your words of comfort and support when I was low. Evang. Juanita, thank you for teaching me how to love myself enough to take care of my health. I also love you for the way you love souls! Keep allowing God to use you to birth souls* in the kingdom. Since this writing, Elder Steadly Mothersill has gone home to be with the Lord. May he rest in peace.

To the saints of Christ Pentecostal Temple, Inc., the Youth Department, and the Mother's Board, who consistently encourage me and support me, thank you.

Evangelist Katherine Palmer, woman of God, my forever mentor and friend, you changed the trajectory of my life with your strong desire to worship the Lord. Thank you for nurturing me and helping me to walk in my calling. I appreciate the way you challenged me. ... It worked.

MY FRIENDS ...

Desiree M. Martin-Hamilton, my best friend in the whole wide world! You are the other part of me. You have been there since I was eight years old, so my life has consisted of you, and I would not change it for anything. You are a remarkable woman, a loving, caring, exceptional mother, and a beautiful light in this dark world. Thank you for seeing the gifts and talents in me when I did not even know they existed and then encouraging me to pursue them. I love you to life.

Rev. Kimberly Batiste, a true woman of God! I love you. When God wanted to decorate the body of Christ, He created you. In my eyes, you are a jewel in the body of Christ, and I thank you for being my friend. I love you, and I appreciate you for your encouragement and support. You taught me how to K.I.M. it!

Dawn Green how blessed I am! You often tell me that I am a blessing to you and your life, but it's the other way around. You have seen me at my high and low points—and you still love me. You understand and know how to separate the evangelist from the person, and you still love me. If that is not God's heart in action, then I do not know what is. Thank you for being my friend!

Min. Stephen Quinones, man of God, you are a blessing to my life. I thank you for embracing our friendship and supporting me. The gift of teaching in you pulled the gift of teaching out of me and out of this came the dynamic duo! Thank you.

Rev. Samantha Lewis, from the time we met, you have been an inspiration to me. Your tenacity, ambition, and standard of holiness are powerful forces. Thank you for being my friend and my sister.

Corey and **Roshawnna Bazemore**, once during my personal prayer time, I asked the Lord to add true friends to my life and ones who I could pour into and see His heart for me through them. Right after that prayer, the two of you waltzed into my life!!! I told God He was showing off because He gave me His finest and most priceless couple. I do not think the two of you will ever understand or know what you have brought to my life. I love you. Thank you for loving me.

Richard Celestin, Esq., and **Elizabeth Celestin, Esq.**, thank you for being supporters of my life and catalysts for my dreams to come to pass. I love you for trusting the counsel and spiritual guidance I give.

Benjamin Rodriguez, president and chief executive officer of the Business Club, you will never know what you mean to me. God has used you to keep my heart on track and push me to go after my dreams. I love you.

A special thank you to ...

Brianna DiDomenico and **Lorena Jacinth,** thank you for letting the light of Jesus Christ shine through you. I do not think that you will ever know what you bring to my life. You have encouraged and inspired me to be greater. Thank you for your contributions to this work.

Bishop Carl E. & Dr. District Elder Dr. Thelma D. Lewis; Bishop Errol and District Elder Judith O'Savio; Dr. Cheryll Holmes; Bishop Eulah M. Nelson & Elder I.V. Nelson; To Bishop Kevin & Lady Norschenia Dobbs and to Nicholas, Nicole, Kevanne and Kary: words cannot express what this family means to me. The anointing and love that flows from you all to the body of Christ is remarkable. To the Women of the **New York State Missionary & Christian Women's Auxiliary,** I love you more than you will ever know. **The Queens Supervised Release Court Representatives** (You make New York's Criminal Justice bail reform work. Without you all, there is no Supervised Release!), **Kathleen Lovell**, the beginning of the Queens Supervised Release Court Representatives, Rest in Peace. My **Soros and Frat brothers of Alpha Nu Omega, Inc.**; My wonderful mentors of Collaborative Experience, Inc., **Julia Shaw & Toni** (Awesome and powerful women, thank you for helping me through the birthing process of this book!); **Mr. James P.** (You are special to me. Thanks for listening to me and being there for me.) **Bahiyjah Morrow; Karine St-Onge,** Creative Director of Shiny Rocket Design. (She designed this cover, Awesome). You are Awesome at what you do, Thank you for your patience, my God Mothers, **Andrea Edwards** and **Margaret Johnson**, I love you both to life! Thank you for supporting me and loving me.

TABLE OF CONTENTS

	PRELUDE	13
Chapter 1	THE PRINCIPLE OF SALVATION—AND SOME OTHER STUFF	15
Chapter 2	THE PRINCIPLE OF SPEECH—A WORD-ACTIVATED KINGDOM	23
Chapter 3	THE PRINCIPLE OF AGREEMENT—NO AGREEING, NO WALKING	31
Chapter 4	THE PRINCIPLE OF UNITY—LET'S COME TOGETHER	37
Chapter 5	THE PRINCIPLE OF ALIGNMENT—LINE IT UP	43
Chapter 6	THE PRINCIPLE OF ORDER—GET AND STAY IN YOUR PLACE!	49
Chapter 7	THE PRINCIPLE OF VALUING TIME—MAKE TIME WORK FOR YOU!	55
Chapter 8	THE PRINCIPLE OF KNOWING—KNOWING IS HALF THE BATTLE	63
Chapter 9	THE PRINCIPLE OF WISE COUNSEL—WE CAN HAVE JESUS AND A COUNSELOR TOO	69

Chapter 10	THE PRINCIPLE OF CHOICE—YOU HAVE POWER TO CHOOSE, USE IT WISLEY!..	75
Chapter 11	THE PIZZA PIE PRINCIPLE—REALLY? I MUST READ THIS!	83
Chapter 12	THE PRINCIPLE OF MENTORSHIP—BE OPEN TO GUIDANCE AND HELP	91
Chapter 13	THE PRINCIPLE OF FIRE—THE RIGHT KIND OF FIRE.........	103
	AFTERTHOUGHTS—IF YOU VIOLATE THE PRINCIPLE, YOU FORFEIT THE PROMISE.................................	111
	REFERENCES	115
	ABOUT THE AUTHOR..	117

Prelude

How? This question has been asked throughout the years. This small, three-letter word has left many people with deficits in their lives. This question poses and pushes the need for instruction. It indicates that we can be stuck if we do not have a set of instructions and directions imparted to us. According to *Miriam Webster's Dictionary*, the noun definition of the word *how* means a question of manner or method. In this book, we will focus on this meaning.

As I sat to begin writing this book, I could not help but think of the many times this question has raced through my mind in my life. The absence of instruction and methodology causes many to lose focus because they do not know how to execute. As a Christian and a lover of Jesus Christ, I have learned that instruction, guidance, and direction are important. This book is designed to walk you through the process of simply learning how to.

The Christian life was designed to be simple, so why is it complex? According to Proverbs 13:15, the word of God declares that the way of a transgressor is hard. The question that then would arise is: "Are all who believe that salvation is hard transgressors?" No, I do not think that's the answer. What then is? We will cover this answer throughout this book. We will learn that salvation is designed to be simple because the cross not only takes away our sins, but it also brings abundant life—a life overflowing with blessings.

With this understanding, we must seek out the simplicity of salvation and walk in it. The question that looms then is, "How?"

We will outline the proper way to apply some of the major themes and principles of the Bible. Reading this book will take the guesswork out of the process of salvation and enable extrapolating a systematic methodology to apply to daily living.

Chapter 1

THE PRINCIPLE OF SALVATION—AND SOME OTHER STUFF

When I received Jesus as my Lord and personal Savior, I thought my life was set forever! I thought I did not really have to do anything but live for God and not mess up. I thought I had it made. What could I possibly have to do to fix my life? After all, Jesus paid it all! I thought my duty was now to read and study His word, live a holy, sanctified life, and be what God called me to be at all costs! Boy, was I wrong!

As I journeyed on this new life of salvation, I began to see life differently. The excitement of salvation permeated my life. All things looked brand new to me. The love in my heart seemed big, and I wanted to please God with every fiber of my being. I was in a church that taught the unadulterated word of God. My pastor was a fiery woman of God! Her call in the fivefold ministry was teaching and being a pastor. She had boldness in the Spirit that was feared by many but embraced by others. She had a phenomenal level of revelation and a deep love for God's people. Her life in Christ was respected, and the anointing on her life was heavily sought after.

One year after I was saved, I was called to the ministry. I literally heard the audible voice of God beckon to me to "feed my sheep." I took this news to my pastor. Her position in my life shifted from not only pastor but also mentor. She began to pour into me the principles of the kingdom of God. Now, at this point, many of you may be asking, "How?" Well, God is a strategic God. He has well thought out plans for our lives, and He leaves no detail to the faulty hands of any man. I make a point to say this because often, when God's plans begin to play out in our lives, we tend to think that they cannot be God.

I'll speak for myself. I began to wonder, "How could God call me to do anything?" Accepting the call on my life catapulted me into a place of darkness. Once I truly said "yes" to the Lord with all my heart and soul, it seemed as if the gates of hell opened in my life. I lost my one and only son, I lost my job, and to top it all off, my marriage was under major attack. Sadness and depression hit me like a ton of bricks. Soon after I accepted the call of Christ, I preached my trial sermon. I even remember the title: "Know Who You Are." In this sermon, the Lord began to tell me to remind His people who they are in Him. The word of God declares that we are "a royal priesthood, a peculiar people, a holy nation." The Lord began to minister to my spirit that we are not ordinary people. He chooses us before the foundation of the world. He impressed in me that we are not like everyone else, and I should remind His people of this very thing.

The Lord further impressed upon me that His people are a priesthood and royalty. These words rang in my spirit. A priesthood represents those of the cloth who serve, yet they are served. Priests understand that they get their fulfillment out of serving others because this is their purpose and destiny. Their level of humility is contingent on how humble they are willing to be. Royalty has to be very cautious and selective about with whom and where they spend their time. Royalty can often be found spending their time with those who are likeminded and striving toward the same goals, dreams, and aspirations they are seeking. Royalty understand the principle that association creates similarity; in other words, who I hang around is who I will be like.

So, it is with the Christians walking with God. We are to be highly selective about with whom we associate. It is okay to have friends who have not yet decided to deepen their relationship with the Lord as you may have chosen to do; however, we must know how to maintain a balance. We must know when to pull back because of the temptation of sin, and we should know how a situation will affect us. Royalty lives a wholly different lifestyle from common people. They are also held to a higher standard. They cannot do what others do. They must always be mindful of their position and what is important yet remain humble.

Not long after preaching this sermon, I lost my job. The first question out of my mouth was, "Lord, how could this happen?" The Lord quickly brought forth revelation. He told me that my trial sermon was the umbrella before the rain. Let me explain. Often, we look at the weather report to see what the weather will be for the week ahead. If the meteorologist says that it will rain on Thursday, we know beforehand to bring an umbrella with us on Thursday. We are prepared before the rain comes.

So it is with the Lord. The word the Lord gave me for my trial sermon was to know who I am—that was the umbrella. Not long after, I lost my job—that was the rain. I had gotten under the umbrella of the word to protect me from the rain of losing my job. This is one way *how* God works. He prepares us for the storm before it comes. The principle that applies here is to know the voice of the Lord. Consider, for example, John 10:27: "My sheep hear my voice, and I know them, and they follow me." He promises many times in His word that He will not have us be ignorant because we will be familiar with his voice as well as with his word (2 Peter 2:38; Hebrews 5:2; 2 Corinthians 2:11).

Many times, we walk around lacking knowledge about our lives because we do not seek the mind of the Lord concerning every area of our lives. The God we serve is not haphazard; neither is He in the upper echelons of heaven, wondering what He is going to do with our lives. We are not an afterthought to God! When God designed us and caused us to be born, He already had a plan for our lives. God is so strategic about us that He designed us for and with a purpose. In Jeremiah 1:5, the Lord states, "Before I formed thee in the belly, I knew thee!" Let that marinate.

When trials, tests, and negative circumstances hit our lives, we tend to think, "*How* could this be?!" In our human minds, we wrestle with the thought that if our God is God, then why is this or that happening? What we as citizens of the kingdom often forget is that the way God works is through principles. If we can understand the concept of principles, we can have much keener insight into what God is doing in our lives. Principles govern the kingdom of God. Herein lies the *how* in the way God works.

In 1 Peter, you find these words: "Beloved, think it not strange concerning the fiery trials which are to try you as though some strange thing has happened unto you, but rejoice, inasmuch as ye are partakers of Christ's sufferings; that, when His glory shall be revealed, ye may be glad also with exceeding joy" (I Peter 4:12–13). I love this passage of scripture because it is literally a map for those facing hot or, according to the way the scripture says it, fiery circumstances in their lives.

This scripture opens with the word "beloved." God is so careful to tell us how He feels about us. He wants us to understand who we are; He literally tells us to be loved. Not only that, but we are also the object in which the love of God is displayed. God, in His infinite wisdom and understanding, wants us to know that no matter what is coming our way, we are loved. The test, trial, or circumstance that is about to or has already hit our lives should not move us away from the love of God. His love is sure, and during what we are going through, His love is strong enough to stand.

This scripture mentioned above goes on to explain how we need to think about our circumstances. Test and trials are not an out-of-the-blue or a strange mishap. This is His way to catapult you to your destiny. It is in the furnace of affliction that God chooses us (Isaiah 48:10), so when fire hits us, He asks us to rejoice.

When I first read this, I could not believe what I was reading. I said to God, "Let me get this straight! You want me to rejoice when fire hits my life?" His response was, "Yes." He went on to explain to me that if I had His perspective on test and trials, rejoicing would be my natural reaction. He is God. He is the author and finisher of my faith. There is nothing that is in my life, is coming to my life, or has passed through my life that He is not aware of and in control of. He knows me and my life, He knows His plans for my life, and He is working in these circumstances to ensure His will for my life. When His will begins to unfold in my life, rejoicing is my reaction because I see His hand at work. Let that marinate as it pertains to your life.

God is no fool. He has an awesome plan for our lives. Life presents many complexities, issues, hurts, pains, sadness, woes, illnesses, shames, and maladies, but we must realize that God uses these things to His advantage. According to Nahum 1:3, the Lord has His way in the whirlwind. Life also has highs: marrying our soulmate, the birth of a child, landing our dream job, buying our first home, taking our dream vacation, and hitting that milestone in our lives. But there is a level of joy that supersedes these, and this is the joy of the Lord! According to Nehemiah 8:10, "the joy of the Lord is our strength." In other words, the joy that the Lord gives remains intact and offers strength no matter what goes on around us or in our lives. The joy of the Lord is not predicated on circumstance. We, therefore, can look at true children of God in the throes of suffering and see that they are joyful. How can this be? They understand that they are God's beloved, and they know that at the end of this, they will be intact, and while going through it, they know it is the Lord's joy that sustains them. Let that marinate.

Notes

Notes

Chapter 2

THE PRINCIPLE OF SPEECH—A WORD-ACTIVATED KINGDOM

Words. There is a theoretical rule according to an article published in *Psychology Today* on September 30, 2011 and to Mehrabian and Wiener (1967) and Mehrabian and Ferris (1967). The rule in Mehrabian and Ferris's study consists of a predecessor formula to the 55/38/7 formula: 60/40. The 60/40 formula compares the importance of the facial (60%) and vocal (40%) components in communicating a person's attitude. The 55/38/7 rule thus give us a snapshot of the power of our style of communication and words. The numbers of the formula represent the importance of the varying communications channels. The belief is that 55% of communication is body language, 38% is the tone of voice, and 7% is the actual words spoken.

Words are important for many reasons. I want to focus on the creative nature of words and how it works. When we ask the question *how*, we must realize that it is such a broad word. It encompasses so much, yet it is small and is often all we can say.

Genesis 1 declares, "In the beginning God created the heavens and the earth. The earth was without form, and void; and darkness was upon the face of the deep. And the Spirit of God moved upon the face of the waters" (Genesis 1:1–2). There was nothing going on. There was void, darkness, and chaos—or, what I like to say, a lack of order and illumination. Nothing happened until God began to speak, and Spirit and word connected. When we get to verse three, we read, "And God said." This is the very first time we see the creative nature of God at work through the vehicle of speech! When God was training me in the power of His kingdom and *how* it works, He spoke these words through my mentor. God's kingdom is a word-activated kingdom! At this point, my mentor had my full attention. God used the power of spoken word to create the whole world. In Genesis 1, everything in the world was spoken into existence. God's labor consisted of speaking. His word is so powerful that it created a whole world!

Now, later in Genesis, God said that He made man in His image (Genesis 1:27). What does that mean? It is God's nature to create. He is a creator. When He made mankind, He did not shortchange us. All men have the ability and proclivity to create, no matter what relationship with God we have. Whether we have a deep relationship with God or not, whether you build on your relationship with God or not, we all have the ability to create because God created all of mankind. All that is in Him is in us, especially if we have the Holy Ghost!

This truth is profound because it means that He has given us the ability to create just like He does. No matter your relationship or lack thereof with the Lord, you have the ability to create. Now, if you choose to cultivate your relationship with the Lord and spend your time building and growing your relationship with God, your ability to create will grow and become sharper as well.

Many times, the world we live in is the world we have created with our own mouths! The kingdom of God is activated by the very words of our mouths. Proverbs 18:21 declares, "Death and life are in the power of the tongue: and they that love it shall eat the fruit thereof." This passage of scripture is the *how* we seek when we learn to utilize the principle of speech. The word power in Hebrew is *yad*; it literally means 'hand' *(Strong's Concordance,* 3027).

The Hebrew mindset behind this definition is that if the tongue had a literal hand, it would come out and begin to create the things you have said. Understanding this idea and school of thought, we **really** must watch what we say! What is the purpose of a hand? What does it do? A hand is used to move things, grab things, set and place things in order, build, and create. Hands usually are the instruments of our actions, whether good or bad. They are used to create and formulate things. With our hands, we can fix, mend, or destroy things. Hands are powerful! So our tongue metaphorically is used and works like a hand. Just like God did in Genesis!

The Creator lives in us, and everything that He is resides in us as well. So, when we say something, we must know that is the world we have created with our own mouths. We, therefore, are not to say things such as "You are stupid," "You make me sick," "I am so ugly," and "I'll never get this right." If we say these things, they are the world in which we will live. Words use space and energy. They hold a spot in the atmosphere until the thing we said manifests.

Another scripture regarding speech is found in Job 3:25: "You shall decree a thing, and it shall be established." Not only is the spoken word important, but so are the emotions, emphases, attitudes, and mentalities behind it that drive it into existence. Imagine what God must have been feeling and thinking when He said, "Let there be light" (Genesis 1:3). Have you ever thought about light? The brilliance, brightness, and penetrating energy of it? Have you ever thought about the speed at which light travels and the ability of light to cut through steel? That is what a laser does. Light is powerful. Do you understand the importance and need for light? Without it, we are in utter darkness.

A lack of light also alludes to a lack of understanding. Have you ever been ignorant or lacked knowledge about something? You metaphorically lacked light. Then, when understanding came, you became illuminated and enlightened or brought light to that issue. The very essence and nature of God can be seen, felt, and experienced in light. So, when He spoke the words, "Let there be light", He put all of who He is into the words He spoke. That same ability is in us.

Another biblical reference to the principle of speech is in the story in Ezekiel 37:1-14, where we visit the story of the valley full of dry bones. Ezekiel was a prophet of the Lord, and according to the scriptures, the Lord carried him away in spirit and showed him a valley of dry bones. As the Lord took Ezekiel through the valley, He was able to see the depth of the bones and that they were very dry. The Lord asked Ezekiel, "Can these bones live?" Ezekiel answered, "Lord, you know."

The Lord's instructions were profound. He said, "Prophesy upon these bones, and say unto them, 'O ye dry bones, hear the word of the LORD.'" (Ezekiel 37:4). According to *Miriam Webster's Dictionary*, the word *prophesy* means to speak under divine inspiration, to preach. The definition of prophecy is profound in the above text because God's instructions were simply to speak. He did not tell Ezekiel to do anything beyond using the principle of speech. When Ezekiel did what the Lord commanded him to do, the bones in the valley connected and stood up and became an exceedingly great army (Ezekiel 4:10).

When this army stood up, the Lord commanded Ezekiel to prophesy again. This time, He told him to call for breath, sinews, and flesh to come upon these bones. The only thing Ezekiel did was speak. He was directed by the Lord to do what the Lord did at the beginning—that is, to speak. When Ezekiel spoke, the bones began to connect to other bone. This is so awesome because the Lord gave no further direction other than to simply speak. As I write this, I love how the Lord allows us to speak to our circumstances and cause them to shift. Our words have power, and it is imperative that we press into the power of our words and use them.

God cannot lie, and He cannot go back on His word. He has declared that to activate His kingdom, a word must be spoken. In Isaiah, these words are penned, "For as the rain cometh down, and the snow from heaven and returneth not thither, … it shall not return unto Me void, but it shall accomplish which I please, and it shall prosper in the thing whereto I sent it" (Isaiah 55:10–11). When rain and snow fall, they change the landscape. They do not return in the same form in which they fell. They begin to work in the ground, providing nourishment to the plants that provide food for us.

This is what the word of God does. When the word of God is declared over our lives and into the atmosphere, it begins to change the landscape of our minds. It cultivates a thinking pattern like God's. When our thinking changes, and we begin to agree with what God has said, we see results. Our world begins to change and transform into the very words that have been spoken. As we push into the principle of agreement by saying what God has said, these words begin to manifest. This is *how* we change our worlds. We speak it into existence.

If you do not like the world you live in, whether your finances, relationships, or career, please know that you have the power to re-create it! By the power of the spoken word, you can create a whole new world to live in. The enemy, therefore, wants to plant negative seeds in your heart and mind, expecting that you will say these things and reap his results in your life instead of God's. It is imperative that we do not speak after the way we feel, especially if our feelings are negative. If we speak these things out with all the emotion we feel while saying them, they are the world we will live in. Instead of speaking our feelings, let's say what God has said about us and our circumstances.

We must also realize that to live the lives we dream about and deeply desire, we must speak out our dreams to ourselves! Now, many of you may feel that this is a bit much, but I say, how badly do you want the life you dream of? How badly do you want to know Christ? How badly do you want to have that thing you want? The Bible declares that faith comes by hearing (Romans 10:17). That principle does not only apply to salvation! It also applies to life! The more you hear yourself saying a thing, the more you will begin to believe it, and the more strongly you will go after it!

When God began training me in this principle, He had me wake up, and before I began any of my daily activities, He had me declare who I am in Him and how He sees me! At first, this was hard because I did not believe any of it. Life had beaten me down so badly and caused me so much pain and hurt that I could not think of myself positively in any way. As I began to say what God said about me, however, I began to see myself the way He saw me. This was the beginning of my healing. Not long after this I began to act like what I was saying, and my world changed! I began to see the very things I had begun declaring. My thinking about myself changed, and my body language began to line up. I found hope, and not long after, my plans were not just dreams but were becoming reality.

I dare you to begin to declare: "I am the head and not the tail. I am above and not beneath" (Deuteronomy 28:13). "I am more than a conqueror" (Romans 8:37). "I am the tongue of the learned" (Isaiah 50:4). "I am the apple of God's eye" (Zechariah 2:8). Yes, Lord! I can literally feel the energy of God while I am typing! By doing this, we activate the kingdom of God, and we live in that world. That is *how* we activate the principle of speech not only in our church life but in all other areas of life.

We must know that we have power. The enemy would love for us to walk around believing that we have nothing to do with our life. He wants us to believe that we are powerless. The enemy wants us to believe that we just have to let life happen to us. He is a liar! God has given us power over ALL the power of the enemy (Luke 10:19)! Beloved, please know that you are not powerless. If you realize nothing else, please know that you have the power to choose. You do not have to stay where you are. You can choose to do something different.

Notes

Notes

Chapter 3

THE PRINCIPLE OF AGREEMENT—NO AGREEING, NO WALKING

"Can two walk together except they be agreed" (Amos 3:3). Often, when we embark on new endeavors, ideas, projects, or anything we aspire to do, we must apply the principle of agreement. Now, in analyzing this scripture, we see the word *agreed*. This implies that we must agree first before we can take another step. Amos asks a question that should cause us to think. I believe if the Bible asks a question, it is not to gain information but to make us think. In my studies and research, I found very little about questions in the bible. The Bible gives great, deep insight into its line of questioning. It is a very powerful principle and is often the reason why many of us lack the success we so desire. In *Miriam Webster's Dictionary*, the word agree is defined as having the same opinion about something or consenting to do a thing offered or suggested by another person.

When we make a conscious decision to go after our dreams and goals, we must make sure that we have come into agreement with someone or something. When we activate the principle of agreement, we allow for accountability and open the way for revelation. Let me explain. In the scripture I quoted earlier, the question is asked, "Can two walk together?" Now, this scripture implies that for two to walk together on the same wavelength or mindset, they must agree first! In other words, you cannot walk together until you agree.

Many of us have issues with God and what He has decreed and declared for our lives, but God will not give us full understanding of our lives until we first agree with Him. Many times, when we ask God, "how?", we do not get the answer because we do not agree. The scripture uses the verb "agreed" in the past tense. This means that we must agree first, and then we walk. Now, the scripture also mentions a number, "Can two?" What two is God talking about? Well, we must first agree that God is right! He is right about the plans He has for our lives, the thoughts He thinks about us, and the feelings that He has for us. Once we agree with God, then He reveals the next step for our lives. When we agree with God, that makes two.

When you begin to ask God about *how* or when you should do this or that but do not receive an answer, check your level of agreement. Agreement brings cohesiveness to what we are working on. Agreement also makes the other parties involved accountable for holding up their end of the bargain. Once agreement is in place, then walking can occur. Many times, we are not able to walk forward in our dreams, goals, and ideas because we have not agreed with God or those He has assigned to our lives and our plans. Agreement deflects the negative energy that comes to throw us off our plans and purpose. It also provides protection when we become weak in our well-doing.

Another application of the principle of agreement is to agree to disagree. In my early days of walking with Christ, I did not understand this concept. When I got saved, I just wanted to go to church, hear the word, and be saved. I did not realize that God had something for me to do. I did not agree that I was to be a preacher. It went against my mindset. At this time of disagreeing with God, I was hurting and angry about the loss of my eight-month-old son. How could I agree with God after He took my one and only child? The hurt and pain were unbearable. My heart and mind were broken in pieces, and God was the last person I wanted to hear from or agree with. During this time, I decided that I would not go back to church. I felt that I had given God a chance, and I was done with Him.

In an attempt to help me save my life, my former pastor asked me to come to church one more time. She told me that if God did not do anything for me that day, then I need not come back again. I agreed with her, and I came. I was so angry and hurt. I was embarrassed, and I could not understand why God would allow this. In my attempt to find an answer from God and to try to put my life back together, I asked God why I had to give up my only son. God's answer was simple yet profound. He said to me that He had given up His only Son for the world. He wasn't asking me to do anything He hadn't already done. He then asked if I agreed with Him. In this moment, I had to agree that I didn't agree with Him, but He was right. Sounds a little confusing, but that was where I was in the process of learning how to agree with God. The key was that agreement was starting to work into place. Despite being hurt and filled with pain, I found a way to agree with God even though I did not like what He had done. Once I began to agree with God, I saw Him move like never before.

I agreed to go to church as my pastor had asked. When I went, God met me there! I sat in the back of the church. That night the message was "Show Me Your Glory." The evangelist preached a word that literally shifted my core! When I realized what was happening and came to myself, the Holy Ghost steamrolled through the church, and I was slain! I began to wail and cry out to God! As I rolled on the floor and cried out to God, I could feel Him lift the pain, hurt, embarrassment, and sadness. In return, the weight of His glory rested in the vacant places of my heart. When I got up, I knew that God had a plan, and I was in full agreement! The anointing on and in my life increased, and the word He put in my belly began to flow. This was the birthing of the ministry on my life, and it was conceived through agreeing with God.

It also allowed me to be open to what He had for me. I could now "walk" with God. Walking implies that we embark on a journey with God. To walk with God, we must agree that He is always right. According to Jeremiah 11:29, He knows the plans He has toward us. Notice that the scripture states "He knows." This means that we must agree with Him to hear His plan and then we can walk. He does not tell us the whole picture because He knows that we do not have the ability to agree with Him. He gives it to us in pieces. This is for our sake because the Lord requires us to agree with Him before we can walk with him. This allows us to walk with God and be in agreement with His plan.

Notes

Notes

Chapter 4

THE PRINCIPLE OF UNITY—LET'S COME TOGETHER

Unity. A small word yet a powerful force! The purest definition of unity, according to *Miriam Webster's Dictionary*, simply means the quality or state of not being multiple: ONENESS, to be made whole. It means being together. In our quest to learn *how*, we must be unified with a cause bigger than who we are. We must unify ourselves with causes and efforts greater than our individuality.

In the book of Genesis, people decided to build a tower straight up to heaven (Genesis 11:1–9). Their desires were birthed out of the great flood and the desire to escape the potential judgment of God. The other aspect of this project was that their leader at that time had literally been embodied by a demonic spirit and wanted his place in heaven back (Genesis 10:10). The people were so adamant and passionate about their cause that God Himself moved (Genesis 11:4)!

Now, the purpose in which they were unified was not in the will of God. For the purposes of this book, though, I want to convey that no matter what purpose we are unified in, God will move. They were not unified for the will of God, but they got results. They caused God to look down from heaven and move. What a powerful force unity is! This lets me know that when we are unified, we can cause God to move. Even though they were negative and contrary to God, they were unified! The principle of unity is the component of *how* that can cause you to move past insurmountable obstacles in your life. When we unify with God, He draws our plans together. Unity links us to the necessary components to bring our plans to life.

When building the Tower of Babel, the people were unified in the wrong cause, but the key was they were unified! The principle of unity was so strong that it caused God to move and do something about it! He *confused* language. You can always tell if the cause with which you are unified with is good for you. A telltale sign is your understanding of the language. When we are seeking the principle of agreement, we must pay attention and learn to hear the language of what we are preparing to do. Remember, we read about the principle of speech earlier. When unity is involved, we must listen to the words we have spoken over our lives and see if those words match up with what we have been saying. As these two principles work in tandem, we begin to see the manifestation of what we are believing. We are then able to see the word of God and the promises of God become reality.

Unity is also the order of God. God is a God of order. He does not work in a haphazard manner. Not only is He a God of order, but He is also very strategic and intentional. The way the Lord has created and allowed events to unfold in our lives is not accidental or just happenstance. Let's look at the creation story. God began to speak, and it was. He started with the heavens and the earth, then light, followed by the separation of the waters from the firmament, and next dry land. Then God called for the earth to bring forth vegetation—grass, herbs yielding seeds, and trees yielding fruit. He next created the light to rule day and night and decorated the canvas we call heaven with stars (Genesis 1:1-18). Notice how God started high and descended. He began up and worked His way down. This order was purposeful. For the fruit and the herbs to come to fruition, they had have light and all of the elements above to function. They also had to work in unity and harmony. They had to work as one whole unit for a common purpose. The whole worked as a unified component for one reason: to glorify God! This is the purpose of unity. Being unified with the plan, will, and purpose of God ensures that He is glorified. If God is not being glorified in **all** that we do, it is null and void; it is meaningless.

Being united with the Holy One, therefore, ensures fulfillment because God *always* works with a greater purpose. From glorifying God, we receive edification and the peace, joy, and fulfillment of knowing that He is pleased. Moreover, as we begin to glorify God, our lives begin to be in alignment with the word of God and true holiness. This level of unity empowers us to be anointed and used by God. It also allows God to entrust us with the divine assignment He has placed in our lives.

We must also be strategic about with whom we unify. As I write this book, the order in which I chose to lay out each principle is purposeful. I believe that the chosen order is the foundation on which we are to execute. With that said, this brings me to those with whom we are united. We are not to unify with everyone who comes into our lives on every level. People are placed in our lives for different reasons and purposes. Our job and assignment is to allow the power and wisdom of the Holy Ghost to lead us and direct us. There are times when God allows a person to be in your life. You are close to them, you share many areas of your life with them, and then something happens, and you two are no longer in relationship with one another. Why is this? How does this happen?

When I experienced this, the Lord explained to me that I did not seek His wisdom concerning the purpose of those whom I let in and out of my life. When God began to teach me the principle of unity, He explained to me that His plan for my life has been intricately woven, and before the foundations of the world, He had me on His mind. At this point, He had my full attention. He explained that it, therefore, was imperative that I be wise about whom I allowed into my life. The Lord further instructed me that when I sought Him, He would allow into my life the people assigned to His purpose and plan for me.

I do not believe in coincidence. I am a firm believer that God orchestrates each part of my life. The people who come into my life must agree with the plan of God for my life. It is part of my divine assignment to include God in every facet of my decision-making.

Notes

Notes

Chapter 5

THE PRINCIPLE OF ALIGNMENT—LINE IT UP

How do we get blessed? Are there specific requirements? Do we need to do anything? The answer to these questions is a resounding "yes." According to *Miriam Webster*, the purest definition of the word alignment is to bring into line or to be in a straight line. You might be thinking, "What does this have to do with *how*?" Well, the Lord God Almighty blesses us in alignment. This means that He has an order for us, and He wants us to be in that specific order before He blesses us. Now, I know many will argue that the Lord blesses them and will bless them in any way He wants. I will not argue with you. This is why it is called a personal relationship with the Lord. However, this does not change the fact that God blesses us according to the alignment of our lives.

When the Lord began to train me in this principle, He imposed upon my spirit that my life needed to be aligned before He could bless me. Needless to say, I really did not know what this meant. Through much prayer and fasting, the Lord explained to me that He does not merely bless us just for us to say that we are blessed. Neither does He bless us for the sake of blessing us. All that God does has purpose and a plan. God is a God of strategy and technique. The word of God declares that the blessings of the Lord make rich and add no sorrow with them (Proverbs 10:22). In other words, when the Lord has declared us to be blessed, sorrow, sadness, hurt, pain, and the like do not accompany the blessing. Because these maladies are not attached to our blessings, this is an indicator for us to recognize how God is moving in our lives. For this principle to be true, God must make sure that we are able and ready to be blessed. I love the Lord because when His name is on something, He always makes sure that it is successful and comes to pass.

The book of Isaiah declares that the Lord's name will not be polluted (Isaiah 48:11). Now understand this: When you were baptized in Jesus' name and filled with the precious gift of the tongue-talking Holy Ghost, the name of the Lord Jesus Christ was attached to your life! This means that His name is on you. With that, you can rest assured that if Jesus promises you anything, it will come to pass. God cannot lie and will not start lying to you. The hold-up is that you are not in line and ready to receive what He has promised.

An example of this principle in my own life comes from when I was asking God for a salary increase. I needed more money and did not want to work a second job. I went to the Lord and asked Him for a raise. About a week after praying this prayer, the Lord said to me that He would give me more money when I aligned myself with receiving more money. I asked God, "*How* could I do this?" He told me to look over my life and see how I was using the money I already had. As I began to peruse through my life, I could see where I was not using the money I had wisely. I shopped as much I wanted, and I often left my bills unpaid. I would pay my tithes and offerings because I believed that my blessing lay in that, but with the other 90%, I did what I wanted to. I bought lunch every day, and I spent money on whatever I wanted. This prayer was prompted because I was facing eviction. My solution to the problem was more money.

In my prayer time with the Lord, He told me the answer was not more money. The Lord began to show me people who made less than me and had way more than me. I'll take you a step further. The Lord showed me people who did not consider inviting the Lord into their finances, but nonetheless had everything they needed. After hearing this, Jesus had my full attention. I went back to the Lord and asked him, "*How* do I do this?" God began to put people in my path who were financial gurus. I began reading books on financial strategies and principles. I began studying biblical financial principles more closely and applying them to my life. I began doing them, not just studying them. I got aggressive about reversing my thinking about my life and my finances. I began to understand that if I was the hold-up in my life, then I needed to make a change. I was tired of my finances being the way they were. I was hearing the testimonies of many who were financially free, and I wanted that. Instead of envying them or complaining that it was too difficult to change, I got with them; I sat down and learned.

After about two months of being diligent with these principles, I received a raise from my job. Once I saw that obeying the principle of alignment worked, I went full throttle with it in other areas of my life. Over the course of the next seven months, I received four more raises! Glory to God! It was working. I was seeing that I had to line myself up with the promises of God, and I had to bring order to my life to receive what God had declared over my life. I also learned that if I had received the raises before I aligned myself, I would have squandered away the money God released to me through my job. More money was not the answer to my eviction issue; wisdom over my finances was the answer.

As I continued to apply the principle of alignment to my finances and other areas of my life, I began to see the hand of the Lord moving. Before, I was not in any shape to receive blessings from the Lord because I was unstable and out of order. God has already declared us to be blessed. We just need to get in alignment to receive it. Aligning ourselves ensures that we keep the blessing and begin to grow and receive other blessings.

Isaiah states that God declares the end from the beginning (Isaiah 46:10). The weeping prophet Jeremiah takes it a step further and says that the Lord knows the thoughts He thinks toward us. Jeremiah further states that the Lord has thoughts of peace, not evil, to bring us to the expected end (Jeremiah 11:29). This is important because when God blesses us, the bigger picture of the blessing is the plan of God. His plan and will are in the forefront of His mind.

Notes

Notes

Chapter 6

THE PRINCIPLE OF ORDER—GET AND STAY IN YOUR PLACE!

The definition of order that suits the purpose of this book is the transitive verb found in *Miriam Webster's Dictionary*: to put in order, to arrange. God is a God of order. Order is important because it is the set-up for other things to come forth. We first hear of order in the book of Genesis, which declares the law of first mention. According to Dr. David L. Cooper's *Hermeneutics: The Science of interpreting Scripture*, the law of first mention is a principle that requires us to go to the place in the scriptures where a doctrine is first mentioned. Once there, we are to study the following occurrences of it to grasp the fundamental, inherent meaning of the doctrine. We can look in the book of Genesis and find the whole Bible in it. However, what we see in the book of Genesis is how it will carry out throughout the Bible.

The book of Genesis opens with, "In the beginning, God …" (Genesis 1:1). As we look at the way God began to create, He started lofty and high with the heavens and the earth. His Spirit began to move on the waters, and this was the first time we see light. He spoke order to the darkness by calling forth light. In other words, illumination brought forth understanding for the rest of creation. As the creation story unfolds, we see the descending order of creation all the way down to the calling forth of vegetation.

Order. For vegetation to grow, it needed light. For the waves and the ocean to move in sync, the moon had to be in place to regulate the tides. If God was this strategic in the creation of the world, how much more strategic is He in the order of our lives? Order is the set-up for the flow of blessings. It is the prelude of peace springing forth in our life.

As I began to study this principle, I realized that I could not function without order. This was so deep in me that I began to see that in my life, I shut things down without order. In fact, I literally delayed a project and did not move if it had no order. This principle began to teach me the detriments of not having order in life.

To understand the power of order, we need to understand ourselves. The lack of order keeps us moving in circles in our own lives. The difference between alignment and order is this: Alignment is making sure that things are in line, whereas order is making sure that the things in line flow when they are supposed to. As in the creation story, God knew that flowers would not grow without light and water; in darkness, what could grow? Light did what it needed to do for plants to grow. This is how God uses order in our lives.

What in your life needs to be brought into order, and how do you plan on achieving this? My journey to bringing order was this: I had to sit down and make a list of the things that were out of order in my life. Even God started with the disorder before He could bring forth order! After He surveyed the situation, He recognized the need for order to come. We see nothing else happening before God brought order. Can you imagine if man had been created first? He would have been in utter darkness! He would have starved and not named the animals! Order is key to receiving and sustaining blessings. Without it, the long-lasting effects of our blessings will die.

Order also serves as the blueprint for us to create new opportunities to spring forth. As we sit down and let order flow in our lives, it is important that we write it down and keep good notes. Our notes should consist of our thoughts, our mindset, instructions and directions given to us from the Lord. This creates our record and proof that blessings are tangible. It also serves as our instructions on how to re-create blessings again.

Order also brings peace. Have you ever noticed that when things are flowing in your life, you are at peace? Peace is often stolen from us due to the vicissitudes of life. Life, in and of itself, has challenges and issues. As you allow order to spring forth in your life, the lack of peace is driven out. Allowing order to come into your life also assists with your thinking. Even our brain thinks in order. Something as simple as numbering pages, saying the alphabet, or realizing that when we wake up, we bathe, clean up, dress, and move on to the day. This all testifies that our brain thinks in a specific order. It, therefore, is imperative that we allow order to come forth and operate in our lives. Order makes our creative nature flow, thus fostering the birth of our blessings.

Wrapping our minds and lives around the principle of order also helps us value our time. Time and money are equivalents in the business world. When persons leave jobs for whatever reason, they have any leftover vacation time given to them in the form of money. One way that we can maintain order in our lives is to learn the value of time. I began to learn the value of time through thinking about recycling. Most things we have can be recycled. We can reuse our clothing, homes, cars, and so on. We can replace these items if we lose them. We can buy them again if for whatever reason we lose access to them. The only thing we cannot recycle is time. I can do nothing about the last five minutes or the past or anytime I have spent or used. The only one who has this authority, power, and strength is the Lord God Almighty. He oversees time from the realm of eternity. When we implement order into our lives our time will be used and spent wisley.

When order operates in our lives, we can actually see, track, value, control, and create our lives by design through the auspices of time. Order as it pertains to time offers balance and steadiness in our lives. It also creates a consistency that lend itself to success in our endeavors. Another step to allow order to operate in our lives is to sit down and track our time. What do you spend the most time doing? Do you take time out of your day to meditate and think? Do you have an order according to which things should flow in your life? Have you written down what you want? Do you know what it takes and how to obtain these things? These things give birth to order. Just like in the book of Genesis, when the earth was without form, and darkness was upon the face of the deep (Genesis 1:1–3), we are without order. What does God do? He starts calling forth order. When we take the time to think, plan, and create in our own lives, we, too, can call forth order.

Notes

THE POWER OF KNOWING HOW | Apply the principle, Get the Results!

Notes

Chapter 7

THE PRINCIPLE OF VALUING TIME—MAKE TIME WORK FOR YOU!

As a counselor talking with many clients, I find that time seems to be a reoccurring theme. In many ways, the need to understand time is great. While many of us understand that there are 24 hours in a day, and we have seven days in a week, we do not understand the value attached to time. Time is a precious commodity God has given all of us. It is an AWESOME gift. Before my relationship with Christ, I really did not know the value of time. I was young, and like most, I thought I had all the time in the world. I felt like I was invincible and believed that what I desired to do would happen later because I had time. It was not until much later in my life that the realization of time and its true meaning became real to me.

The way in which God began to help me to understand time was this: We are all given 24 hours in a day and seven days in a week. Whether we are rich, poor, black, white, red, yellow, educated or not, employed or not, young or old, whatever our culture or background, we all get the same amount of time. When I began to realize this, many questions began to rise in my head. Why then are some of us poor, and some not? Why are some educated, and some not? Why do some enjoy life, while others struggle? The Lord began to speak to me, and He said this, "I give all the same amount of time. The real question is: What have you done with the time I've given you?"

Let's look at time according to Psalms 90:10: " The days of our years are threescore years and ten; and if by reason of strength they be fourscore years, yet is their strength labor and sorrow; for it is soon cut off, and we fly away." According to this scripture, we are given 70 years. Now, in our day and age, people are living to be centenarians. This makes my point even stronger. If we look at our time to live from, let's say, 70 years, and we break that down, this is what the time in 70 years looks like:

> 70 years = 839.999 months
>
> 70 years = 25,550 days
>
> 70 years = 613,200 hours
>
> 70 years = 36,792,000 minutes
>
> 70 years = 2,207,520,000 seconds

WOW! When we look at time from this perspective and compare it to the span of a lifetime, we have no time to waste. God oversees time. He knows us down to the very second and has a plan for our lives planned out in every detail. Many of us spend our time doing things that do not matter, things that rob us of our time. Meanwhile, we are still responsible for fulfilling the call and plan of God's will in our lives.

I really began to ponder this. Warren Buffet has 24 hours just like you and me. What has he done with his time that allows him to have the life he has? Mother Theresa had 24 hours in her days like you and me. What did she do differently? The great Rev. Dr. Martin Luther King, Jr., had 24-hour days and seven-day weeks like us. What did he do to obtain the results he got? Now I know many of you may be saying, well, these people had different circumstances than I do. While that might be true, one common denominator remains: They all had the same amount of time you and I have.

The Lord further told me that to understand the importance of time and how it works, we must know that our choices and decisions on what to do with our time are the key to how we value our time. According to Forbes Magazine's 2018 list, Warren Buffet is the third richest man in the world. How did this happen? What did he do differently? Now some may say that he was born rich or has always had money, and this may be true. However, to keep and maintain his financial status and grow his riches, he had to have a plan, he had to have order, and he had to know what to do with his time. I am almost sure there were days when Mr. Buffet did not feel like getting up out of bed or studying six hours a day. Maybe some days, he wanted to just sit back and enjoy his riches and not think about crunching numbers or reading financial reports. However, he understood this: What he does with his time determines what his life and his future will look like. Notice that I did not say "his past." Mr. Buffet understands that he cannot do anything about his past. The only thing he can do is learn from it and adopt the principles that worked.

Now, please know that I understand that we are all born in different circumstances. Some of us come from places that are horrific. Some are born in extreme poverty and highly dysfunctional families. Some are born with every odd against us and do not even know there can be a different life. I understand these things, but I also understand that when we grasp the power of time and how to use time wisely to make healthy decisions, we can have any life we desire.

When I decided that I wanted an awesome life, I began to evaluate and take inventory of my life. Overall, I have had a good life. I grew up in a loving family with both my parents in the home. I am the baby of the bunch and was and still am doted on by my family. I was sheltered and protected from many things, and I know this was done out of love. It created a curiosity to know and explore things. When I was about 18 years old, I began to explore and seek outside the boundaries and parameters my family set.

Needless to say, this threw me off track in my life. I went to college and graduated, and the next step would have been law school. Well, in the time between graduating and applying to law school, I met a guy, got married, and got pregnant. My whole life changed in what seemed like an instant. I was thrown off my scheduled plan, I was out of order, and my time was off. Instead of re-evaluating my life, setting order, and getting back on track, I just let life happen. When I came out of this season, I was divorced, had lost my eight-month-old son, and was sick and broke. This was a very difficult time in my life. I felt so alone and distraught. I did not know if I was coming or going. I was living from day to day and letting things just happen. If I felt like doing this or that, I would, and if not, I just did not do it. I lived by my emotions and had no regard for time.

My take on time was that when I get around to it, I'd do it. Or I just thought that I had time and could do it whenever. I seemingly forgot that time marched on and waited for no man. While I sat there thinking that I had all the time in the world, and the sun rose and set around me, I wasted valuable time. I could not get back the time I lost. I could not change things that I did in the past, nor could I go back in time and change any decisions I had made. This realization hit me like a ton of bricks. When my son passed, I was in a state of mourning. I felt like it was unnatural for a parent to lose a child. I was suffering from a psychosis, and as the days turned into night, I was oblivious to time. I did not eat. I did not sleep. I did not talk. I did not bathe. I did absolutely nothing. I could not reconcile in my mind a loss of this magnitude.

It was my pastor who invited me back to church and asked me to give God another chance. I agreed and went to church. That night, the word from the preacher was "God, show me your glory!" The preacher began to talk about how Moses had asked God to show him His glory. God told Moses to get up early in the morning and hide himself in the cleft of the rock. The Lord further told Moses, "I will put my hand over your eyes, and when I pass by, I will separate my fingers and allow you to see my glory" (Exodus 33: 18-23). The preacher spoke and said that many of you sitting here today, are between a rock and a hard place, but God wants to show you HIS glory. God wants you to know that the hard place you are in is designed not to destroy you or kill you but to foster and grow your relationship with Him. She said that it is time for you to see the glory of the Lord!

Well, in that moment in time, I had a decision to make. I could stay in my hurt and pain and continue to mourn the loss of my only child, or I could make a decision to go after God and see Him high and lifted up. It was a hard choice because everything in me wanted to wallow. I felt justified in my emotional pain. Can you imagine the pain my heart was in? My only son, my baby, was gone. I would never hear him call me mommy or see him take his first step. I would never see him go to school or get married. In that moment, my life was over.

God, in His infinite wisdom, grabbed me out of the abyss of depression. He spoke the word that utterly changed the trajectory of my life. He said, "Nikka, I know you are hurt, and I know the pain that is in your heart, but please understand that I have not allowed you to suffer any pain that I have not experienced. I am with you in this place. Also, know I gave up my only Son for the sins of the world." In that moment in time, I could feel the pain and hurt in my heart lift. I began to see the bigger picture of what the Lord was trying to accomplish in my life. I did not have all the answers nor did I know what I should've been doing, but I knew that I had to make a decision, and this was the time.

Had I stayed in that place, I would have died. Time was marching on. Things were happening and changing. Life did not stop because I had suffered a tragedy. The Lord began to coach me through the fact that I still had work to do, and I still had something to offer. I was still responsible for everything He put in me, and the world needed it. Was I still hurt? Absolutely! In fact, I will never get over that loss. When my son died, a piece of me died. I had to learn to live with it. The operative word being LIVE; I could not merely exist. While I understand that we are all different and process our circumstances differently, we must realize that we all have the same common denominator to work with: time.

Notes

Notes

Chapter 8

THE PRINCIPLE OF KNOWING—KNOWING IS HALF THE BATTLE

So what do you know? While this seems simplistic, I find that a lack of knowledge has been the culprit in many downfalls. Hosea 4:6 states, "My people are destroyed because of a lack of knowledge, and because you have rejected knowledge, I will reject you." God desires us to know. He also *requires* us to know. According to *Merriam-Webster's Dictionary*, the word know means to; understand and to be acquainted or familiar with.

Knowing a subject means being cognizant about it. When studying the word *know*, I found many different definitions. While the definition quoted is the one I want to focus on, I want to briefly look at the definition of *know* as to be intimately acquainted with.

In Matthew 7:23, we read these words: "And then will I profess unto them, I never knew you: depart from me, ye that work iniquity." This verse has always fascinated me because one attribute of Christ is that he is omniscient, or all knowing. This begs the question of how, if God is all knowing, He could not know me. As I further researched the word *know* in this text, I learned that here, it means to be intimately acquainted with. It speaks to intimacy and sexuality. Now understanding that He is God, and He knows everything and everybody, I began to grasp that He was referring to an intimate, deep relationship with Him.

Yes, God has knowledge and is cognizant of us and who we are, but God also desires to know us up close and personal. The idea here is that God wants to be involved and invited into every aspect of our lives. He wants to be included in our daily activities as well as major events in our lives. Inviting God into all areas of our lives allows us to know Him and His nature. Now, I understand that we can never exhaust God and His infinite wisdom, but we can become familiar with how His spirit moves.

As I reviewed the intimate sense of the word know, I realized that when we are intimate with God, when we bask in His presence, when we sit at His feet, when we walk into His bedchamber and lie with Him, He impregnates us with His word, essence, power, attributes, and glory. When we come away from being intimate with Him and knowing Him on a deeper level, we are now able to give birth to the things He has impregnated us with. This idea excites me because when two people are in love, and they make love, they create offspring. The principle of being intimate and knowing is powerful.

The aspect of knowing is simply the power of knowing. One of the best ways I can describe this principle is this: Let's say that you have a pearl. It is huge and beautiful to look at. The iridescent glow that shines off this pearl is eye catching. Now, this pearl has been passed down in your family for years. Your great-grandmother gave it to your grandmother, who in turn passed it down to your mother. One day, your mother pulled you to the side and gave it to you. She told you that this pearl is special because it has been passed down through the family for years. She did not tell you how much it is worth or where it came from, just that it has been passed down in the family.

You may not have full knowledge of the pearl, so you put it in your jewelry box for safekeeping and leave it there. It is not until one day that you peruse through your old jewelry and keepsakes that you come across this pearl. Out of curiosity, you take this huge, beautiful pearl to a jeweler to have it appraised. To your astonishment, you are told by the jeweler that this pearl is worth thousands of dollars! The jeweler looks at you trying to see if you understand what you have. Realizing that you now know what you have, the jeweler begins to downplay the value of the pearl. He says, well, it's old and has suffered some wear and tear. He even suggests that he can take it off your hands if you want him to. Your response is to quickly grab your pearl and make a mad dash for the door.

Now, had you known the value of this pearl, you would have more deeply cherished it. Before the appraisal, it was simply a pearl from your great-grandmother. While it had sentimental value, you were not aware of what you really had. After you learn its value, your whole thought process and mindset change. You begin to think hard about your future. You begin to realize that there is a shift about to take place. Even your personal value and assets increase. The person you were before gaining this knowledge about the pearl is different from the person you have become.

Now that you are aware of what you have and know that it should be handled with care, you go full throttle and do it. Well, this is how we need to act when we gain knowledge, information, and wisdom. These are the pearls the Lord allows to come into our lives and lead us. In the scripture quoted earlier, Hosea 4:6, God literally rejected those who rejected knowledge. Knowing is what will allow us to make well-informed decisions and healthy choices.

In the pearl analogy, once you know what you have, your whole thinking changes. The Lord always desires our thinking to change to the way He thinks. Isaiah 55:8 states, "For My thoughts are not your thoughts, neither are your ways My ways, saith the Lord." In other words, God knows that our thinking capacity cannot compare to His. His thoughts are lofty, high, and exalted. Through His omniscience, He can see all the pieces of the puzzle, all the possible outcomes, and know what will work in our best interest.

I often think about the fact that God chose me, knowing everything about me. He knew all of my downfalls, all of my hang-ups, the times I would disobey Him, and the times I would doubt Him. He knew what I would struggle with and how those things would affect me. Knowing all of this, He chose me anyway! This absolutely blows my mind. Not only did He still choose me knowing all of this, but He also loves me through it all.

For this reason, we should have a mind to know God and cherish the wisdom He has given us. Proverbs 2:6 states, "For the Lord giveth wisdom: out of His mouth cometh knowledge and understanding." God understands knowledge and wisdom, and that the ability to apply knowledge is the "how to" in many life situations.

Notes

Notes

Chapter 9

THE PRINCIPLE OF WISE COUNSEL—WE CAN HAVE JESUS AND A COUNSELOR TOO

Early in my walk with Christ, I learned the power and necessity of wise counsel. When I lost my son, my insurance company required that I attend professional counselling. I was very reluctant to do this because I had learned that many in the church were against counselling. It seemed that there was stigma against counselling, and if you consulted with a counselor, you did not trust God.

To be in accordance with the rules of my insurance company, I attended counselling. It was a big shock to me. It was a great experience and an eye opener. When I attended, one of the biggest lessons I learned was that I was not alone. The room was filled with women and men who had lost a child or multiple children. While this brought a sense of relief, it was also very sad. Many of the women and men were what we called veterans in losing. They had been in this group for ten years or more and were very well able to assist us newcomers.

I looked around that room into the eyes of men and women who had lost children. For some, the pain and hurt was fresh, as if the loss had just happened. Some had learned how to live with it and were very much able to help us get to the point where they were. The common denominator among all of them was that counselling was the key. They all stated that in some way, shape, or form, counselling was the key to their healing. We had sponsors assigned to us, which allowed us to reach out when we needed to talk to someone or needed someone who understood exactly where we were. As I continued to attend counselling, I realized how much I needed it and how much of a process counselling was. I learned that while the loss of my child was the surface hurt, there was so much more hurt, pain, sadness, and despair underneath. As the layers began to be peeled back, I could see how much more I needed and wanted to further explore counselling.

This was the beginning of God's call on my life to be a Christian counselor. I could not wrap my brain around the loss of my son, and I had many, many questions for God. While I was going through this, I had people in church coming up to me and saying things such as, "You'll be okay. You're young enough to have more children." "You could not have been too attached to him. He was just a baby." "Just trust God. You'll get over it." These words haunted me daily. I could not believe the way people thought, that they had the nerve to verbalize these words. It drove me into a shell and made me very defensive. I did not know how to guard my heart or deal with people. I became agoraphobic and began to build up walls and defenses to protect myself.

As I was seeking to be emotionally healed, the Lord opened a door for me to take classes in Christian counselling. I did not even know that it was a thing. I knew about counselling, but I never knew that Christian counselling existed. As I matriculated through the classes, I learned that counselling was real and sanctioned by God. The Lord himself began to open my understanding regarding counselling. He explained to me that *counsel* simply meant wise advice, a safe place to be emotionally naked and not worry about being judged. The scripture He backed this up with was Proverbs 11:14: "Where no counsel is, the people fall: but in the multitude of counsellors there is safety." As the Lord talked to me, this freed me to trust in the gift of counselling.

He further supported this by allowing me to excel in my studies. My professor, Dr. Robert Hines recognized the gift of counselling in my life and that I was able to assist others through the counselling process. He often told me that I was very patient with those who were in crisis or had suffered trauma and needed guidance. He pushed me and mentored me. Sitting under his tutelage helped me understand why counselling was so important to me. I realized that I was able to provide people with what I needed and wanted while I was going through my hard times. I wanted to know how to navigate through my emotions. I needed to understand that what I was going through would end. During my suffering, I often felt judged, afraid, and very concerned about what people thought and said. I decided that if I were ever in a place to help someone through a hard time, I would be the opposite of what I had experienced. I wanted to provide a safe place for people to come and get help without judgement. As I went through the counselling process, I learned that counselling was a necessity in the lives of God's people.

As I began to learn more about counselling, I had more and more questions. Why are so many in the church against counselling? Why are so many of God's people depressed, sad, and miserable? Why are they not eager to learn how to live in the now instead of the past? Why are they afraid to hear the truth? The Lord helped me to understand that counselling is like an onion. As people begin to peel back the layers of their lives, it makes them cry, but it reveals the truth. He further explained that the layers are like people's past, and sometimes it is easier to just leave the past alone than deal with it.

I am so grateful for learning about Christian or faith-based counselling. The Lord pushed me and beckoned me to keep going. Through this experience, He birthed in my spirit my faith-based counselling practice. I learned the power of providing a safe, warm, inviting, clean space for His people to become emotionally naked. I learned that God is a God of hope, and He wants us to be conduits spreading hope to others. He also explained that counselling is a way to evangelize to those who need to have a deeper understanding of who He is.

Through my experiences and my practice, I have helped many come to a place of wholeness. In John 5:6, we read, "When Jesus saw him lie, and knew that he had been now a long time in that case, he saith unto him, "Wilt thou be made whole?" Notice that He did not ask the man with the infirmity if he wanted to be healed. The first time I read this passage, I did not catch this, but the Lord instructed me to go back and read it again. The Lord helped me understand that healing is being free from one's physical ailments, but being whole means the whole being—mind, body, soul, and spirit. This man had been in that state for a long time. He laid there making excuses for why he never tried to get whole. When Jesus came, He changed the whole trajectory of the tradition.

According to the scriptures, the tradition was whoever got in the water first when it was troubled was healed. When Jesus came, He never put the man in water. Instead, He talked to him; He counseled him. The man never got in any water, but he received his healing and wholeness. He had a conversation with Jesus that caused him to think deep within himself. The excuses he had used for so many years came face to face with the truth. He could no longer hide behind them; he had to deal with them. He could not say that this was too hard, or he did not have the discipline to change. When he answered Jesus and decided to believe Jesus, he was made whole.

Jesus instructed him to take up his bed and walk. When I think of my bed, I think of a comfortable, warm, cozy place. My bed is decorated with beautiful pillows and always smells like fresh linen. To me, my bed is also the place where I decide to rest and lay a little longer, making excuses to move later. This man could no longer live with the excuses that he lived with for so long. Counselling supports us in facing our truth. It allows us to understand that comfort zones can become dead zones. This man was now free to walk in a place where he could be free of excuses, live in truth, and enjoy life. Go ahead, and visit my website, so you can be like this man and be whole.

Notes

Notes

Chapter 10

THE PRINCIPLE OF CHOICE—YOU HAVE POWER TO CHOOSE, USE IT WISLEY!

Have you ever thought about what goes in to making choices? As the Lord impressed this thought onto my spirit, I began to think about it. The ability to make choices is very powerful. In Genesis 2:17, we read that God told Adam that he could eat from every tree in the garden except the tree of the knowledge of good and evil. The Lord told Adam what would happen to him if he ate from this tree—he would surely die.

In Genesis 3:6, we see that Adam ate. Adam decided to disobey God, knowing what the circumstances would be if he did so. As I think about this, I shudder. Adam knew what would happen to him if he ate. Adam made up his mind to disobey God, followed the lead of his wife, and ate the forbidden fruit.

The ability to choose is one of the most powerful tools mankind has, in my opinion. I have often heard people say, "Well, they made me do it." "I really did not have a choice." While I understand what they mean, this is not true. While we may not like what we must choose from, there is a choice. Many argue that if a person has no place to live and no form of income, they do not have a choice but to be homeless and beg as a means of supporting themselves. I argue that choosing between going to a shelter or sleeping on the street is not pleasant, but when you think about it, the person may be safer in the shelter than on the street.

Many times, in high school, I heard a classmate say, "She made me do this or that." The parents replied, "So if they tell you to jump off a bridge, would you do it?" In other words, do you not have your own mind? Are you not capable of making your own choices? Sometimes, it is so much easier to blame someone else for what we do not want to have a hand in choosing.

The ability to choose is a precious commodity. By profession, I am a forensic social worker in the New York City Queens Criminal Court system. As I talk to my clients who face exuberantly high bail, the one thing they often say is that they regret the decisions they made before being arrested. Now, many are arrested for things they have not done. Some are wrongly accused, and in this circumstance, they understandably did not have a hand in being arrested. However, those clients who knowingly participated in illegal behavior and are now looking at having their freedom taken away wish they had made better choices. As I interview them to help with their release, they began to trace their thought patterns that led to the decisions they made. They can literally trace the pathology of what they were thinking and why. They say things such as "If I would have just decided to go a different way." "I wish I would have not decided to go there this day."

Many things can be taken from us, but choice is always available. As I read the writings of the great apostle Paul, I am always in awe of where he was when he wrote many books of the Bible. He was often in jail. These jails were not equipped with televisions, comfortable beds, gyms, libraries, and access to programs—no. He was often bound hand and foot. He was in pits that had fecal matter on the ground. The stench was horrible, and food was scarce. There, Paul decided to write letters by which we as Christians govern our lives today. He wrote the profound message stating that he counted all he had suffered as nothing so that he could win Christ (Philippians 3:5–6). Paul choose to not let his circumstances make him. Sure, he could have said, "This is just too much." He could have said, "I am of the tribe of Benjamin and was circumcised on the eighth day." He could have said, "I have a covenant with Abraham. I do not need to go through this," and decided to go back to the life he once lived. But, no, he didn't.

Paul understood that because God had chosen him, he now wanted to choose God. Paul knew that his suffering was not worthy to be compared to the glory that would be revealed in him. He understood that if he chose God, he could never go wrong. Romans 8:28 says, "And we know ALL things work together for good, to them that love God and to them are the called according to His purpose." Paul understood that the power to choose was influential. He did not give away his ability to choose to circumstances he did not like. Paul had his mind and eyes set on achieving the end results and pleasing God. This drive inside him outweighed the environment around him.

This must be our stance. In my opinion, anything that robs us of the ability to choose is completely wrong and not for us. Even God, in His omnipotent wisdom and omniscience, does not stop us from choosing. He gives us the details before we choose, but He does not stop us from choosing. As referenced, Adam made a conscious decision to eat the forbidden fruit. God told Adam what would happen before he decided to eat it, but he chose to eat it anyway.

I have learned that I have an enormous power in my ability to choose. Things do not just happen to me. I have a say in how things play out in my life. I do not have to just sit down and take things that come my way. I can exercise my ability to choose, and that is great power. This principle was driven home when I lost a job for the first time. This was a job I did not especially like, but it was in my field, and I wanted to grow. Around the same time, I had been saved and was super-excited about serving God. It seemed as if every other week, there was a trip or an event to attend. Often, these events were during work hours and required taking time off work.

I decided that I would learn more about God by going to these events. I was super-excited. I would call my job and simply say, "I will not be in this weekend or this day." After about four months of doing this, I called one day and said I would not be in this day. The voice on the other end said, "OK, and please do not report on Monday. Your assignment has ended." I froze looking at the phone and thinking to myself, *What just happened?* It took me about ten minutes to realize that I had been fired. My initial inclination was to blame somebody. I wanted to lash out because after all, I was serving God, and if my job was in the way of me knowing God, He would take care of me. I was so wrong.

It was not until much later that I realized I had chosen to be in that place. The decisions to not go to work cost me my job. I spent three years and eight months unemployed. I was educated, had a degree, had graduated with honors, and had significant experience. None of that mattered. I was immature in my decision-making, and I did not realize that I could not do what I wanted to do simply because I had the ability to choose.

Through that period of unemployment, I learned to cherish my ability to choose. It is a power given to me by God, and like I cherish all the other wonderful gifts He gives me, I cherish this as well. I learned that taking the time to think is precious and can save much heartache. If I had simply taken the time to think about how being unemployed would affect me, I might have chosen differently. Many of you may be thinking that was a no-brainer. Why would you jeopardize your job? Please understand that I came from the church era when you did what you were told. While my leaders did not decide for me, they heavily influenced my decisions. They were very hands-on and involved in my life. There were other ways to learn God, but at the time, my eagerness and emotion got the best of me. God does not allow His character to be polluted by our choices. He has provided us with everything we need to live an abundant life. I cannot blame God for the choices I made.

Learn that choosing is not easy, but it is simple. When you are about to make a decision, think first. Learn to think critically about the situation in front you. Think about it from every aspect. Ask yourself questions. How will this affect myself, others, and my family? Learn to wait. Sometimes we must process what we are thinking about. This takes time. If you need to, talk with someone who is full of wisdom and can help you think. Make sure this person will not tell you what you want to hear but will tell you the truth. This is a great start to learning how to make healthy choices.

Notes

Notes

Chapter 11

THE PIZZA PIE PRINCIPLE—REALLY? I MUST READ THIS!

One day when I was at work, my boss walked into the office. My boss and I were very close. We shared many special events together and highly respected each other. I admired him for all he had accomplished at such a young age.

That day he came into the office, I was depressed because I was contemplating divorce. I had many reservations. I was an ordained minister with New York State and the Pentecostal Assemblies of the World. I was an evangelist. I preached and taught all over the United States and abroad. I helped people fix their lives through my counselling services, and I was a personal cheerleader for my clients. The stigma in the church against divorced, single, female ministers is unbelievable. I knew that if I divorced, I would be treated like a second-class citizen of the kingdom of God. I was very afraid to get divorced because I did not want to face being alone, especially in the church. The mindset of those in church can be cruel to single people, and I did not want to deal with this.

Moreover, this was the father of my son who had preceded us in death. We had been through so much already, and I really wanted my marriage to work. I had always wanted to get married. I grew up in a home where both my parents were present. I saw the power of having both parents participate in raising their children and guiding the home. I wanted that. My parents were my greatest examples, and my family was and still is my greatest cheerleaders.

When my boss and I were talking that day, I began to confide in him how I was feeling. I explained all of these circumstances and how I knew I needed to make a decision. I had a husband; I was okay. It was like my husband was a placeholder, so I would not have to face all of the circumstances I feared. I had decided that I would just stay in an unhealthy marriage and live in that negative environment. This was the day that I learned that not choosing was a choice.

After I had finished pouring out my heart and feelings to my boss, he looked at me and gave me this profound analogy. He said, "Nikka, if you have a whole pizza pie, and you remove a slice and put pasta in the place of the slice you took out, it is no longer a whole pizza pie." He further explained that the pasta fills the place of the missing slice, but the pie is not whole. This shook me to my core. At that moment, my mind was illuminated. I had held onto my marriage to simply keep my husband in place, so I could say that I was married, but it was not a healthy marriage or the marriage I desired. My husband was just holding a place in my life, but my life was not whole. It was just filled!

As I went through the day, I was in deep thought about what my boss had said. I began to think about other areas in my life that had placeholders. What excuses was I using as pasta, keeping my life from being a whole pizza pie? Many times, making a choice requires that we face the things that cause us fear and angst. In an attempt to not deal with the looming fears our choices will yield, we make excuses. This is the "pasta" in our "pizza pie." As

As I continued to ponder my boss' words, I could not help but think of how many things I had backed down from. As I perused through my life, there were so many instances when I had made an excuse instead of making a decision. Over the next few months, I really sought to remove the pasta and the placeholders out of my life to make a whole pizza pie. I quickly learned that Jesus is a safe way out.

This whole train of thought was driven by fear and simply not wanting to deal with the circumstances in my life. When we embark on a journey to become whole, we must first deal with the pieces of our lives that are fragmented. These missing pieces rob us of living a whole, robust life. I have learned that life is like a puzzle, and many fragmented pieces need to be put in place.

I wanted so badly to be whole, but my life had big, chopped-up edges hanging off. I was accustomed to smoothing those edges over. I had learned the art of masking things and making it look like everything was okay. In my head, if the slot was filled, I was good. This approach is dangerous because eventually, the reality of the situation surfaces—along with all the attached emotions. Another alarming aspect of living like this is that reality becomes distorted. It becomes difficult to know the difference between what is real and what is not. Not only do you have to deal with what is buried, but you also have to deal with all the emotions attached to it. The mask or the placeholder of excuses robs us of being whole. We must learn how to deal with the circumstances that life gives us and not back down from them. Doing so is not always easy, but it is very necessary. We must take advantage of the time allotted to us to deal with the fragmented pieces of our lives.

After this important principle was downloaded into my life, I decided to act. The first thing I did was thank God for not leaving me ignorant. It was a harsh truth to deal with, but it made me free. Once I made a decision, I realized that I was taking action and becoming whole. The next thing I did was to write down all the areas of my life that needed to be made whole. I worked on ten areas:

1. What do I want to do with the rest of my life? Develop a vision statement and my brand. What do I want to be known for? What problems do I want to be remembered for addressing?

2. My vision for my spiritual growth and development

3. My vision for health and fitness

4. My vision for companionship and marriage

5. My vision for my family, both immediate and extended

6. My personal vision for my ministry, business, and professional career

7. My vision for my financial stability and soundness

8. My vision for my friends and colleagues

9. My vision for my personal growth and development

10. My vision for rest, refreshing, renewal, and personal recreation

The title of this book is *The Power of Knowing How, Apply the Principle, Get the Results*. I do not want to shortchange you as the reader. I want to share with you what I did and the above is one of the formulas that I used. I want to give you a guide that can assist you in navigating your own life and getting the results you desire to see. These areas of my life made up my being. They were the essence of who I was, and they defined me. After close examination of my life, I could see that I needed a lot of work.

After identifying each area, I wrote what I wanted to see in every area. When I was done, I had a 22-page report on my life. I went into full detail. Doing this forced me to think. It also taught me that thinking about my life was necessary to ensure success.

I then proceeded to create a vision board, keep a gratitude journal, and wrote down affirmations. I confessed my affirmation out loud every day. The word of God declares that faith cometh by hearing and hearing the word of God (Romans 10:17). I then began to meditate on my vision board. I also applied scripture to everything I did.

Habakkuk 2:2 states, "And the LORD answered me, and said, 'Write the vision, and make it plain upon tables, that he may run that readeth it.'" At the time I was doing this, vision boards were very popular. I did not want to do what everybody else was doing but to be in alignment with the word of the Lord. It was as if I were starting a new life, like I had a second chance. I wanted to make sure that this time, I would do all that I could to make the rest of my life be the best of my life.

Another step I took was to meditate on God's word every day. I also allowed myself to dream again, to feel my dreams. With the loss of my son and the dissolution of my marriage, I had given up on dreaming. I felt like any dreams I had were dead and never to return. I had placed so much pasta in my life to fill in the missing pizza slots that I did not even recognize my own life! I began to seek out mentors for each of the ten areas in my life, and I worked hard to get a whole pizza pie life.

The meditation and the vision board helped me focus and see the life I wanted. The affirmations built up my faith and prepared me to fight for what I wanted, and the word of God was what I stood on and continued to live by.

This process took a lot of work. There were days that emotions would rise to the surface. To get what I was seeing in my head, I had to work past myself. I was my biggest obstacle. I had spent so much of my life making excuses and putting things off. Procrastination combined with fear, doubt, and a lack of resources were the challenges that had almost destroyed my life. They had done a number on me and almost won.

Thanks, be unto God for loving me enough not to leave me the way I was. Through these steps and with the help of the Lord, I was able to turn my life around. I began to think of myself as an asset and a precious soul. My thinking about myself and my life literally changed, and I fully believed it, so I was able to work on it. My life was becoming a whole pizza pie.

Notes

Notes

Chapter 12

THE PRINCIPLE OF MENTORSHIP—BE OPEN TO GUIDANCE AND HELP

THE POWER OF MENTORSHIP

From the Heart of District Elder Rev. Judith O'Savio—The Mentor

Being a mentor is an awesome gift from God and a humbling experience that should not be taken lightly. A mentor is someone who guides another person on a journey that God orders and ordains for both the mentor and the mentee. As a mentor, I am honored that my mentee accepted me as God's tool in her life. I didn't see it coming, but as I reflect, I think about qualities that my mentors gave to me. In my life, I've had five mentors, some in my early youth, young adult life, and even this day. If we are in tune with the will of God for our lives, we can be guided on the greatest journey of our lives with mentors whom God strategically places in every stage of our lives.

To me, a good mentor is faithful to God, committed to God, and knowledgeable about the word of God. A good mentor is dedicated to people, helpful to people, and loves people as God loves them. My mentors have shared these characteristics with me, most of them unknowingly. One of my mentors was my second-grade teacher. She was my first African-American teacher whom I was blessed to know as a child and now as an adult. She proved to be a great role model and fully committed to the youth, people, and God. Another mentor was my band teacher who shared his faith. He was a fine musician who through his dedication, passion, and discipline inspired a community of pied pipers to be excellent in everything they did. My aunt was a mentor to me and instrumental in developing my resolve to be a teacher, study, and love people. Another friend was a mentor in how to be a lady, minister's wife, and women's leader in the church because we are powerful prayer warriors and soldiers in this army of the Lord. Finally, my mother, 101 years young at the time of this writing, is in sound mind and able to live an exemplary, holy, dedicated, faithful, loving life. I am so glad that she can still pray for me and give me sound advice.

When looking at Exodus 18, we see Moses, who had a good relationship with his father-in-law Jethro, accepting sound advice. It is so important to live our lives with good character and integrity, so that when the time comes for us to be used by God, there are no obstacles in the way of us being effective mentors. Moses was judging from morning until evening, spending a huge amount of time and energy with the people. Jethro gave Moses sound advice, telling him to be the leader, go to God in prayer on their behalf, teach them the word of God, and show them the way they are to live and how to behave. Jethro also told Moses to select capable men from all the people, men who feared God, who were trustworthy, and teach them to be judges. What a blessing for Moses to recognize what Jethro was saying to him!

As we have faith in God to give us mentors, we must have faith in God to take advantage of their advice and guidance. Some guidance may be by example; some guidance may be words of wisdom. Some advice may be words we do not want to hear or cannot understand because of what we are going through, but if we are led by the Lord, we should be thankful for the direction of the Holy Spirit through those mentors. We should be thankful for the mentors in our lives.

Thank you, Reverend Nikka Williams, for claiming me as one of your mentors. It is an honor and a privilege.

From the Heart of Nikka Williams—The Mentee

You are more than welcome, District Eder O'Savio. I love you to life.

One of my first entryways into serving and working in the church and the kingdom of God was the New York State Council of the Pentecostal Assemblies of the World. The churches I have attended are members of the Pentecostal Assemblies of the World, which is broken into diocese and districts. We have assigned bishops over each diocese. We are further broken into councils by state.

When I first came to the church, my then-pastor was the former state women's president of the New York State Council of the Pentecostal Assemblies of the World. She served two consecutive, four-year terms. She was a phenomenal president. She set the bar high for those who followed in her footsteps. During her presidency, many women and men received deliverance and freedom in their lives through the power of God. The information delivered during our meetings was life changing and memorable. When I came to the New York State Council, people were still talking about her tenure as president. After I received salvation, my pastor immediately put me to work in the council. I started serving on committees. In my church, I was the secretary for four different auxiliaries. My pastor believed in being kept busy.

Unbeknown to me, she was preparing me and mentoring my life. Before this time in my life, I did not understand the power or principle of mentorship. I did not know what mentoring was about, and I did not know its value and importance. As I began to serve the women of God and sit at their feet and learn the ways of the Lord, I was introduced to District Elder O'Savio. When I came to the council, she was vice president of the New York State Missionary & Christian Women's Auxiliary. The president then was Evangelist Dr. Mable Nelson. She was a PHENOMENAL woman of God. She unapologetically walked in the power of the anointing. Even with all that anointing in her life, she remained a lady. She knew her place and understood her position as a wife, mother, preacher, evangelist, and child of God.

As I watched her from afar, I secretly admired her. She seemed regal in her position as president. During one session, she looked right at me and said these words, "One day, you will be president of this auxiliary." Now, this was the second time I had heard this. My pastor had prophesied these words and immediately began grooming me for the position.

Well, election time came around. I believed the women of God who had prophesied about the position of president in my life. I knew they were on point, but honestly, I was not interested. I just wanted to be saved. I was young in the Lord, and I really did not understand the power of serving in the kingdom of God. As I served on various committees, my secretarial skills began to develop and become known throughout the council. When it came to the position of secretary, I was the only one nominated. For the office of President, District Elder O'Savio was the only one nominated. We both went into office unopposed.

You can imagine my shock and amazement. This series of events was the beginning of my mentor–mentee relationships. I began to learn the power of mentorship through my relationships with these women. Now, my first mentor was my mom, of course. She was my first teacher of the Lord. She instilled the foundation of Christ and a relationship with Him in me. She put the word of God in front of me and always encouraged me to serve in church. Even though I strayed as I got older, the foundation she put in me was the catalyst to bring me back into relationship with Christ. Through the various mentors God placed in my life, I began to see the foundation my mom instilled in me grow and mature as I worked for the kingdom of God. I truly thank God for a mother who knew God and raised me up in the ways of the Lord.

I served as secretary of the New York State Council for eight years. I was the youngest woman to serve as secretary for this auxiliary in the council's history. I was 27 years old when I began to serve. Under the leadership of District Elder Judith O'Savio and her mentorship, I learned how to serve in the kingdom and move in the church, letting the spirit of excellence guide me.

Now, our relationship was not set up by my request for her to be my mentor or hers to be a mentor in my life. The Lord showed her what had been prophesied in my life, and she began grooming me, pouring into me, and teaching me. One key to this relationship was that I had to be humble and submissive enough to receive what she was giving. When we met, District Elder O'Savio had held seven offices on the state level and was the wife of a prominent district elder, who was the secretary of the council and went on to be the chairman. She served as the executive pastor at her church and had been a successful teacher for more than 30 years. With this pedigree, she could certainly guide my life.

What made the idea of having her mentor me so successful was her willingness to pour into me and my willingness to receive. Not only was she a successful servant in the kingdom of God, but she also loved the Lord. In every fiber of her being, you could see her love for God. As I began to serve, I realized that I wanted what she had. I wanted my life to reflect my relationship with the Lord. I wanted God to know me intimately. I wanted Jesus to take pride in the way I served Him. This was where mentorship came in. I did not know how to obtain all these attributes on my own. The desire to have all these attributes visible in my life was not enough to possess them. I needed to sit and learn the ways of the Lord, His principles, and His attributes. I needed to learn how to apply His principles and get His results. I needed to see what loving God looked like.

Mentorship was Jesus' way. Mentorship is visible throughout the Bible. We see Moses mentoring Joshua, we see Elijah mentoring Elisha, we see Elizabeth pouring into Mary, and of course, we see Jesus raising up and mentoring the twelve disciples. Jesus loves us so much that He does not leave the task of fulfilling His will in our lives up to us. He assigns mentors to us. Now, the old Zen proverb states, "When the student appears, the teacher will show up." We must ever be students because this is the way we get taught.

The Bible states in 1 John 2:14, "I have written unto you, fathers, because ye have known Him that is from the beginning. I have written unto you, young men, because ye are strong, and the word of God abideth in you, and ye have overcome the wicked one." God depends on the knowledge of those who are older and those who have travelled through life's journey to lead and assist those who are younger and preparing for the journey of life. Mentors are designed to assist us in the journey of life and prepare us for the assignments in our lives. A mentor can be a person close to you or someone who you may not even know. Often, a mentor-mentee relationship develops organically. We do not usually ask someone to mentor us; instead, it develops out of a need we have and a mentor possessing a quality to help fulfill that need.

When the Lord began to teach me about the power of mentorship, He explained to me that I should gravitate toward those doing what I desire to do. He further explained that to receive from my mentors, I needed to remain teachable. When God called me to the ministry as an evangelist, my immediate response to the Lord was "no." I did not know what it meant to be an evangelist, and this caused a great level of fear in my life. My pastor explained to me that the Lord would teach me and encouraged to remain open to His leading.

Of the many attributes District Elder O'Savio possessed, she was an evangelist. She was known as a student of God's word, very eloquent in speech and possessed a steadfast, fasting life. She was a true worshipper and was always careful about the way she represented the kingdom of God. She had an anointing to gather God's people, which is a direct attribute of an evangelist. As I humbled myself and became more open to the call on my life, the mentors I needed began to appear.

Through serving as the secretary of the New York State Missionary & Christian Women's Auxiliary, I learned how to work in the kingdom of God.

I learned much about God's people, His heart toward them, sensitivity to the Spirit of God, and how to move when he said move. Seeking the mind of the Lord for information that would edify His people and what He wanted His people to hear was a key. I learned that if I was not going to work with excellence, then I should not be working.

As I watched District Elder O'Savio preside over the women of God, I began to see how to go in and out before the Lord. She prayed and fasted for what the women of God needed. She worked tirelessly to make sure that the programming before God's people was what He wanted and they needed. At the same time, she knew how to remain in her place as a pastor's wife. She never usurped authority over her husband and did not mind a position of submission.

In our services, the vice president would invite President O'Savio to step up to the pulpit and carry out the rest of the service. Stepping up to the pulpit, she proceeded to follow the protocol of the house. In our organization, it is customary to acknowledge and honor those in leadership positions. She started from the state diocesan and worked her way down to the children in the service. When she was done with the protocol, the roaches in the room felt important. She possessed such a grace and an anointing to acknowledge the call of God on the lives of His leaders and all His people. When she finished, she had set the tone of the service, and the Lord would steamroll through it. The power of God was so great because order was set. She took the office of president very, very seriously. She always said that she was working as unto the Lord, and her assignment was to serve God's people.

As I watched her, I began to look over my own life and examine where I needed to improve. I took mental notes of what she was doing and how she moved. I began to pray that the Lord would help me to be all He called me to be. When one begins to submit to mentorship, when you first start walking in your calling, you often look and sound like your mentors. You often adopt their mannerisms, and you may act like them, talk like them, and even walk like them. As you continue to walk with the Lord and submit to His will in your life, you come into your own about who God has called you to be.

Mentorship is designed to show us the way and to help us in the journey that God called us to walk. In 2 Kings 2, we find the story of Elijah and Elisha. The prophet, Elijah performed seven major miracles in the Bible and was known for his radical approach to performing miracles. Elijah had his ear inclined to heaven and walked in total obedience to God. His experiences with God were miraculous in nature. He was known for being brave and having great expectations from the Lord. When Elisha came on the scene, he was enamored by Elijah. He began to follow Elijah and watch how he moved. Elisha desired to serve God but lacked an example. He had the same call on his life as Elijah but was not ready to walk at that level of depth in anointing. Elisha needed a mentor. This is how his relationship with Elijah began.

In 2 Kings 2:9, we see that Elisha asked Elijah for a double portion of Elijah's spirit to be placed upon him. Now, Elisha made this request when he knew that Elijah would be taken away from him. This was the end of their journey, and it was time to pass on the mantle and place the anointing on the mentee. The Bible records that Elisha performed 14 miracles—exactly double the number of miracles Elijah performed.

To be able to perform these miracles and know what to do, Elisha had to sit and learn. The time he spent with Elijah was training. In response to Elisha's request, Elijah replied that he could have it if he saw when Elijah left. This meant that Elisha had to watch Elijah. Elisha could not sleep or take a break. He never knew when his mentor would be taken, so he always needed to be ready.

President O'Savio and her administration served two terms, followed by an extra year at the pleasure of the diocesan. Election time was approaching. It was time for the nomination process. Nominations were made, and I was nominated for the office of president unopposed. The prior seven years were my training to be president of the New York State Missionary & Christian Women's Auxiliary. I am the youngest sitting president in the history of this auxiliary. None of this would have happened if I had not sat through the series of mentors that God assigned to my life. It started with my mom and is still going on today. As stated, when God called me to evangelize His kingdom, I did not know what that meant, and I did not want to do it. In my pastor's godly wisdom, she understood that I needed teaching, and she began to teach me. God also knew that I wanted to obey Him, and He knew what my reservations were.

In His infinite wisdom, God sent Evangelist Katherine Palmer into my life who literally held my hand and taught me what it means to be an evangelist. She taught me that evangelists are those who gather God's people. She also taught me the power of worship. We met at my church. I admired her from afar and enjoyed her lifestyle of worship until the Lord opened a door for us to attend a yearly retreat.

During this time, she taught me about evangelizing and the true meaning of being an evangelist. I watched her spend hours and hours before the Lord in worship and prayer. I remember seeing her dance before the Lord and cry out to Him for more of His presence. She taught me how to rightly divide the word of God and master the call on my life to evangelize. She often called me in the middle of the day and shared what God had revealed to her. The revelations God shared with her caused people to go after God with everything in them. I remember she preached the power of God so strongly that people fell out under His power. I saw all this, and I wanted it. Our relationship was the catalyst that pushed me forward in the call on my life. It energized me and ignited a fire inside me that still burns today. As I write and reflect on our relationship, I marvel at how the Lord showed His love for me in this way. He literally put someone in my life who would be patient with me until I could grasp His will and run with it. God is good! Like Elisha, I asked for it, and she said to me: if you want it, go after it.

Mentorship is the epitome of a relationship with God. I have had many, many mentors. I have learned that mentorship is the way of God, and He ordains it because it is one of His ways of ensuring our success in Him. Be on the lookout, and search for the mentors you need in your life. The call on your life depends on it, and your destiny awaits you.

Notes

Notes

Chapter 13

THE PRINCIPLE OF FIRE—THE RIGHT KIND OF FIRE

Fire. Fire is a true phenomenon. We experience fire in many ways. We cook our food with it. We sit in front of a warm, glowing, cozy fire and enjoy its heat and warmth. At campsites, fire is used not only for cooking but as a source of light. Many have sat around warm fires and shared numerous stories that have shaped the fabric of their lives. Fire can be the catalyst that brings people together and brings out their inner essence. Fire can be awesome.

Fire also has another side. We often hear about and are well aware of its destructive nature. Many have been the victims of its ability to harm and destroy our lives. Often, depending on the level of destruction caused by fire, the victims have to rebuild their lives and start over. The destruction of fire forces them to work and get moving. They have to find the strength and power to continue in life after losing all they have.

As it is in the natural, so it is in the spiritual. Fire in our lives does the same from the spiritual perspective. The keys to navigating spiritual fires are our attitudes and perspectives while going through fire. God does not allow spiritual fire to destroy us. If God wants to destroy us, He does not have to use spiritual fire to do it. Often, when Christ sends fire into our lives, He is drawing out what is buried in us. Fire is one of the tools Christ uses to get what is in us out onto the surface of our lives.

As I think about this principle, I am reminded of some fires in my life. During the writing of this book, this chapter was born out of a situation that surely was a fire to me. I was praying and asking the Lord to help me with my attitude. The Lord had blessed my life tremendously, and I was and am eternally grateful and thankful for His many blessings. However, as I looked over my life and thought about His holiness, I began to analyze my life and ask Him where I needed work, what areas of my life needed improvement. Through prayer and fasting, He began to show me my attitudes.

I love God and His people. I love serving God's people through ministry and being available. To serve God and His people, attitude is extremely important. As I sought the Lord about the self-inventory I was undertaking, He began to show me how my attitude was killing my growth in Him. My own thinking and behavior held me back. As I continued to pray about it, the Lord showed me that He was ready to help me with it, but I was not ready to let it go. As the Lord and I went back and forth about it, my attitude remained the elephant in my life, stunting my spiritual growth.

Now, no one just wakes up one day with a bad attitude. It comes from somewhere. In my case, it was part of a defense mechanism. My attitude was the cloak I used to hide my fears, hurt, and anger. I truly wanted the Lord to help me with it. That meant that I had to be willing to let down my guard, trust the Lord, and let Him do the work. I had to be vulnerable before the Lord. I had to be emotionally naked. This was hard and almost impossible for me, so in His loving kindness, the Lord sent fire.

You may be asking how He did that. Here, let me tell you. I had been working in the vineyard of the Lord for a while. Compared to my mentors and predecessors, my time was yet short, but I did have a little time under my belt. In the time I had been walking with the Lord, God had allowed many advances in my life, for which I was (and am) humbled and grateful to Him. After 19 years, I went back to school and obtained my master's degree and licensure as a pastoral counselor, and I had three thriving businesses. However, none of these things mattered without the right attitude, a humble attitude. Now, I thought that I had a level of humility. These accomplishments were great, but they meant nothing without the right attitude. They were access points. While working on these accomplishments, the Lord sent my mentors to remind me that humility was a journey with no destination. In other words, I needed to be prepared to go lower if necessary.

Through my accomplishments and my work, I began to mentor many people. We talked and studied together. I poured some of these same principles into their lives, and they got the desired results. It was great! Now here came the fire.

One mentee whom I trained and poured into got promoted above me. When this happened, I could feel the fire shooting through my body! I felt like I would crumble into ashes right in my office and just die. I could not wait until I got home to talk to the Lord, so I went to the bathroom. When I got in that stall, I said, "Lord, what is this?" He immediately responded to me and said, "Your attitude demoted you. I sent this fire to help burn it out of you and help you grow, so next time, you will be ready."

I was totally blown away. On one hand, I was devastated, but on the other, I was grateful. My mentors always told me that you can freeze by degrees—in other words, God does not need your education to advance you or move you, so do not rest all your expectations for advancement on that. My mentors further explained that without the right attitude, nothing in my life would change.

In that bathroom stall, God had my complete, undivided attention. He further spoke and said, "Go back into the office, with a smile on your face. Congratulate her, and thank Me for loving you enough to help you." He said, "Your attitude is based on how you respond when you do not like the events that are happening to you."

After about thirty minutes of crying, I did as I was instructed by the Lord. While devastation had rocked my mind and heart, a sense of relief flooded me. God had rescued me from myself. I was destroying my own life with my horrible attitude and did not realize it. It was self-sabotaging behavior. Have you ever sensed that you should be further but do not understand why you are not? Or have those around you grown, but you have not advanced? You could be holding up your own advancement. Now, God does have a set time to advance us, but we must be ready when that time comes.

This fire was the RIGHT kind of fire!!!! I needed this fire. Over the next few weeks, I got moving! I did not realize that I was stuck in place because of my attitude. I was fossilized by my own thinking and behavior. THANK YOU, JESUS, FOR SENDING THE FIRE! As the weeks went on, the Lord ministered to me. He explained to me that He allowed this to happen because my bad attitude could not go where he was taking me. He further stated that He allowed this to happen down here, so that when I got to where He was taking me, I would be prepared. Now, all of this was not my fault, and the enemy had his hand in it as well. He wanted me to react negatively. He wanted me to forsake God and be angry. Those who worked against me had a hand in it as well. They expected and wanted my demise and bad attitude. This situation was a great opportunity to the let the light of God shine through me.

I started this chapter by talking about the destructive nature of fire. In this test, I learned that all that is burned by fire is not bad. I needed those bad attitudes, negative, horrible thinking, fear, anxiety, hurt, and pain to be burned out of my life and my spirit. I needed the light of God to shine through me. The fire that God sent burned out the things that hindered me from being all He intended me to be. This fire also burned away the thinking that caused me to be stuck in my life. In this test, I learned that much of the fear and anxiety I was experiencing was due to not doing what the Lord had called me to do.

The Lord instructed me to add this chapter in my book, and He told me to push my businesses forward and stay close to Him. That fire in my life was what I needed to get in alignment with the Lord's plans for my life. It was the right fire. I put this book on hold for a while, but now you are reading it. This was the RIGHT KIND OF FIRE. The Lord instructed me to add this last chapter and get this book out. This was the RIGHT KIND OF FIRE. My businesses are thriving and growing. This was the RIGHT KIND OF FIRE. I have humbled myself and know that I have room to go lower. This was the RIGHT KIND OF FIRE. I am learning and intend to master my responses to the things that happen to me that I do not like. This was the RIGHT KIND OF FIRE.

Notes

Notes

Afterthoughts—If you Violate the Principle, You Forfeit the Promise

During one of my many prayer times, the Lord spoke these words to me, "Nikka, if you violate the principles that I have set forth, you forfeit My promises." Now, when these words hit my spirit, I was stuck. I needed the Lord to open my understanding and explain to me His mind and heart. This is how the title of this book came about.

The Bible is filled with promise after promise for God's people. God loves to see His will fulfilled in our lives. The Bible declares in Luke 12:32, "Fear not, little flock; for it is your Father's good pleasure to give you the kingdom." God does not want to just bless us; He wants us to have THE KINGDOM! The Lord loves to see us blessed, healthy, and our souls prospering (3 John 2:1). He loves when we are walking in His divine will and in faith. Just like any good father, He loves to shower His children with the gifts of peace, joy, happiness, fulfilled purposes, divine destiny, and revelation. God gets pleasure in blessing His people.

One obstacle that keeps us from walking in God's fullness of blessings is that we do not honor His principles. Principles are necessary to govern the trajectory of our lives. God gives us principles so that we can receive His promises. Please understand that if God speaks a word, declares His principles, and puts forth His will, He will not go back on it. When words come out of the mouth of God, they begin to create. God does not override His spoken word. If He declares a word, it will come to pass.

This is also true for His principles. His principles must be followed to receive the promises of God. As you read this, go over your life, and see where you may have violated, misunderstood, or simply not recognized the principles of God. As you do this, pray and ask the Lord to guide you. As He leads you, be sensitive to the leading of His Spirit, and obey His voice. As He shows you where you need to obey and apply His principles, do it. I promise you that your life will never be the same. Your BEST life awaits you!

Notes

References

Miriam Webster's Dictionary. (January 1, 2016). Merriam Webster Inc. Springfield, MA.

Mehrabian, A., & Ferris, S. R. (1967). Inference of attitudes from nonverbal communication in two channels. Journal of Consulting Psychology, 31(3), 248–252. http://dx.doi.org/10.1037/h0024648

The Holy Bible. (2016). King James Version 1611, Authorized Version. Zondervan.

Strong's Concordance, 3027 - Yad.

About the Author

Rev. Evangelist Nikka A. Williams, B.S., MSW, *loves the word of God and intends to declare it with power and authority! Through the ministry God has bestowed upon her, many have been delivered and set free from the bondage of sin and darkness.*

On April 6, 1999, Nikka was baptized in Jesus' name and filled with the Holy Ghost at the Agape Church of Apostolic Faith, Inc. Her mother was her first teacher of God and was adamant about living a God-centered life. Nikka's wisdom and knowledge of the Lord were further instilled by the late Pastor Patricia Ann Hayden Newton. In April 2001, Nikka was called to the ministry. On July 15, 2001, she was locally licensed by the Pentecostal Assemblies of the World and delivered her trial sermon. In October 2008, Nikka was instructed

by the Lord to move her membership to Christ Pentecostal Temple, Inc., where Bishop Dr. Derrick Farmer, DD, is the senior pastor. She currently serves as an associate minister. Through practical teaching and life-changing preaching, Bishop Farmer continues to train and instill the principles of God in Nikka's life.

Nikka is an ordained minister with the Pentecostal Assemblies of the World. She currently serves as president of the New York State Missionary and Christian Women's Auxiliary, leading more than 500 women in the ways of Christ. She has also been appointed as the Assistant Parliamentarian and Chairlady of Programming of the International Missionary & Christian Women's Auxiliary with the Pentecostal Assemblies of the World.

In 2013, the Lord enlarged the territory of Nikka to entrepreneurship with the launch of Go, Grow & Glow, LLC, a faith-based counselling and wellness practice. It specializes in the reintegration of a healthy lifestyle and adoption of a holistic approach to counselling. Through this business venture, her clients have spanned America and the seas to Japan. In late 2019, Nikka will release her first published book, which aligns with the counselling treatment she provides.

Nikka completed her professional studies for a Bachelor of Science degree in criminal justice from St. John's University and a master's degree in social work from Stony Brook University, graduating cum laude. She furthered her education with the National Christian Counselors Association, receiving her pastoral counselor licensing.

Nikka has been employed by the New York City Criminal Justice Agency for the past nine years as a court-based social worker. The New York City Criminal Justice Agency provides pre-trial services for the City of New York, as well as statistical information based on arrests throughout the city. In 2009, the New York City Criminal Justice Agency piloted Supervise Release, an alternative program to detention. The success of the program has saved New York City more than $35 million and allowed more than six thousand clients to fight their cases while conducting their lives outside Riker's Island. Nikka has played an integral part in the success of Supervise Release as she has advocated for more than seven hundred clients to receive the program's services before *several judicial justices.*

Within her community, Nikka is active and busy about the Lord's business. In the summer of 2017, Nikka was inducted into the International Christian Sorority of Alpha Nu Omega, Inc., in which she serves as historian on the executive board. In March 2018, which is known as National Women's History Month, Nikka was honored by Beautiful Men & Women's Magazine as a phenomenal woman in her community. In July of 2018, Nikka was certified as a life coach by Dr. Cheryll Holmes, a certified trainer of the John Maxwell Team School of Life Coaching. Through this certification, the Lord has added wellness coaching, mentoring, master class training, and webinars to her already thriving business. TO GOD BE THE GLORY FOR THE GREAT THINGS HE HAS DONE!

If you desire faith-based counselling services, assistance with mental health, seminars, workshops, training, motivational speaking engagements, or life coaching, please contact Nikka at www.gogrowandglow.com *or email her @* nikka@gogrowandglow.com.

Thank you for supporting this work. May the Lord richly bless you.

Have you made Jesus your Lord and personal Savior? Are you looking for an awesome worship experience?

If so, please come and worship with us at Christ Pentecostal Temple, Inc. We would love to have you. Our worship services are truly an experience! We are located at:

Christ Pentecostal Temple, Inc.
109-45 157th Street
Jamaica, NY 11434
(718) 529-3900

Saturday Morning Prayer 7:00 a.m., Sunday Morning Prayer 9:00 a.m., Sunday School 9:30 a.m., Sunday Morning Worship 10:30 a.m., Monday Noon Day Prayer, Monday Night Prayer 8:00 p.m., Wednesday Noon Day Prayer, Wednesday Night Bible Class 7:30 p.m., Friday Night Youth and Evangelistic Service 8:00 p.m.

Nikka A. Williams loves and supports those who pursue their dreams. Please visit the evangelist at www.gogrowandglow.com

www.ingramcontent.com/pod-product-compliance
Lightning Source LLC
Chambersburg PA
CBHW052058070526
44584CB00017B/2241